The Book on "Mt

"This book was written using 100% recycled words."
- Terry Pratchett

With over 1,500 Quotes and jokes we are sure you will find that perfect inspirational quote.

I would like to dedicate this book to all my friends and family that are standing behind me while I do this crazy book writing thing. I would also like to dedicate it to all the people that have been quoted in my books. Without their insight, foresight, and general sense of humor this would just be another book quoting a bunch of boring people.

Other books recommended by Neal Ranzoni
The Shit Neal Has Said and Done By Valerie Moore
Sustenance By Nate D. Burleigh
Nasferas Book One: The Begotten By Nate D. Burleigh
The Orphanage By Amy Crowe
The Father- Time Machine By Sean Dudley
Secrets Unbound by Malissa A Hall
Secrets Found by Malissa A Hall
Bound By Torment By Nancy Baker

The legal junk I was told needs to be in place:

If you have time also check out other books by Neal Ranzoni

"Coming Out" The Guide To Acceptance
"The Shit My Boyfriend Says And Does" (About Neal Ranzoni)
"Naming Your Baby For Success"
"The Suicide Handbook"
"God Knows All. Neal Knows Everything" Coming 2013
Terrie Rideout`s Crock-Pot Cookbook
Terrie Rideout`s Diabetic Cookbook

The Book on Quotes Series
The Book on "Art Quotes"
The Book on "Death Quotes"
The Book on "Education Quotes"
The Book on "Friendship Quotes"
The Book on "Happiness Quotes"
The Book on "Humor Quotes"
The Book on "Inspiration Quotes" Vol. 1"
The Book on "Inspiration Quotes" Vol. 2"
The Book on "Leadership Quotes"
The Book on "Men Quotes"
The Book on "Money Quotes"
The Book on "Motivational Quotes"
The Book on "Music Quotes"
The Book on "Relationship Quotes"
The Book on "Religious Quotes"
The Book on "Science Quotes"
The Book on "Sex Quotes"
The Book on "Truth and Honesty Quotes"
The Book on "War Quotes"
The Book on "Wisdom Quotes"
The Book on "Women Quotes"
The Book on "Writing Quotes Vol. 1"
The Book on "Writing Quotes Vol. 2"

"The rock and roll business is pretty absurd, but the world of serious music is much worse."
- Frank Zappa

"Somebody get me a cheeseburger!"
- Steve Miller Band

"Our music is our alchemy."
- Saul Williams

"Many roads to take some to joy some to heart ache"
- Kate Winslet

"Where words fail, music speaks."
- H. C. Andersens

"With the truth, all given facts harmonize; but with what is false, the truth soon hits a wrong note."
- Aristotle

"We're hotter when we don't give a damn."
- Butch Walker

"Because there's beauty in the breakdown."
- Imogen Heap

"Every hidden cell is throbbing with music and life, every fiber thrilling like harp strings."
- John Muir

"Rush to danger; wind up nowhere."
- Morrissey

Then you'll see the glass, hidden in the grass."
- Morrissey

"Yeah, you're a regular Mozart...well, except for the whole music thing."
- James Dashner

"And all of those who sing on-key, they stole the notion from you and me."
- Morrissey

"Why don't you find out for yourself?
"If everyone started off the day singing, just think how happy they'd be."
- Lauren Myracle

"In the hall itself the din of the music - for this is the real way to play a jukebox and what it was originally for - was so tremendous that it shattered Dean and Stan and me for a moment in the realization that we had never dared to play music as we wanted, and this was how loud we wanted."
- Jack Kerouac

"The art of music is good, for the reason, among others, that it produces pleasure; but what proof is it possible to give that pleasure is good? If, then, it is asserted that there is a comprehensive formula, including all things which are in themselves good, and that whatever else is good, is not so as an end, but as a mean, the formula may be accepted or rejected, but is not a subject of what is commonly understood by proof."
- John Stuart Mill

"Rock'n'roll is a teenage sport, meant to be played by teenagers of all ages--they could be 15, 25 or 35. It all boils down to whether they've got the love in their hearts, that beautiful teenage spirit."
- Michael Azerrad

"All I can do is read a book to stay awake, and it rips my life away, but it's a great escape."

- Blind Melon

"There's somethin' 'bout the way the street looks when it's just rained. There's a glow of the pavement. You walk me to the car and you know I wanna ask you to dance right there in the middle of the parking lot. Yeah."
- Taylor Swift

"Poetry is the language of the soul;
Poetic Prose, the language of my heart.
Each line must flow as in a song,
and strike a chord that rings forever.
To me, words are music!"
- Lori R. Lopez

"Isn't this enough? Just this world? Just THIS?"
- Tim Minchin

"I wanted to paint a picture some day that people would stand before and forget that it was made of paint. I wanted it to creep into them like a bar of music and mushroom there like a soft bullet."
- O. Henry

"Ruling piano keys is harder than ruling a whole kingdom."
- Yazan Haddadin

"Oh! to shoot for the stars if feels right. Aim for my heart if it feels right."
- Maroon 5

"Kids on the Youtube, learning how to be cool."
- Toby Keith

"Owls hoot in B flat, cuckoos in D, but the water ousel sings in the voice of the stream. She builds her nest back of the waterfalls

so the water is a lullaby to the little ones. Must be where they learn it."
- Karen Joy Fowler

"I'm either hopelessly misunderstood or an idiot."
- Raine Maida

"Speaking unspoken words, music is a good way to say."
- Toba Beta

"When I was a child, Mama had the best voice of all the members of the church. She had loved to sing. Her words had soared like an angel's over the swells of the organ. In fact, I now suspected, her entire theology had been taken from the hymnal."
- Siri Mitchell

"The old man slowly raised himself from the piano stool, fixed those cheerful blue eyes piercingly and at the same time with unimaginable friendliness upon him, and said: "Making music together is the best way for two people to become friends. There is none easier. That is a fine thing. I hope you and I shall remain friends. Perhaps you too will learn how to make fugues, Joseph."
- Hermann Hesse

"He stilled my room, for sure."
- Suze Rotolo

"These songs tell me I'm not alone. If you look at it that way, music...music can see you through anything."
- Hannah Harrington

"I'm the hero of the story, don't need to be saved."
- Regina Spektor

"I wish the government would put a tax on pianos for the incompetent."
- Edith Sitwell

"A long apprenticeship is the most logical way to success. The only alternative is overnight stardom, but I can't give you a formula for that. "
- Chet Atkins

"Music and comedy are so linked. The rhythm of comedy is connected to the rhythm of music. They're both about creating tension and knowing when to let it go. I'm always surprised when somebody funny is not musical."
- Conan O'Brien

"You know, people can't fall in love with me just because I'm good at what I do."
- Robert Plant

"I just happen to comprehend the low standards of the majority of the music-buying public, and I don't care how condescending that sounds, it's true. They always go for the shiny gimmicks. Always."
- Tiffanie DeBartolo

"I would say that music is the easiest means in which to express, but since words are my talent, I must try to express clumsily in words what the pure music would have done better."
- William Faulkner

"You all have a gift. It's free. It's the gift of song."
- Christine E. Schulze

"Say it loud and sing it proud today."
- Noel Gallagher

"Music is a world within itself, with a language we all understand."
- Stevie Wonder

"The music was more than music- at least what we are used to hearing. The music was feeling itself. The sound connected instantly with something deep and joyous. Those powerful moments of true knowledge that we have to paper over with daily life. The music tapped the back of our terrors, too. Things we'd lived through and didn't want to ever repeat. Shredded imaginings, unadmitted longings, fear and also surprisingly pleasures. No, we can't live at that pitch. But every so often something shatters like ice and we are in the river of our existence. We are aware. And this realization was in the music, somehow, or in the way Shamengwa played it."
- Louise Erdrich

"She was famous, and she was insane.
Her voice soared out over the audience, holding them spellbound and enraptured, delivering their hopes and fears tangled in chords and rhythm. They called her an angel, her voice a gift. She was famous, and she was a liar."
- Dianne Sylvan

"The chef who cooks without a song on his lips cannot hope to infuse the right carefree improvisatory note into his art."
- James Hamilton-Paterson

"My mind begs for you in the soft, secret, silent places of the night... I thirst for you and without you my soul is a desert. I thought when I first met you, first saw you, that I loved you more than any woman had ever loved a man, but now I know the feeling only grows within me. You are the song I sing each day, each moment, each second. You are the melody of my life..."
- Gloria Smith

"I want to write a song about one man's level of commitment called, "I'd walk to the edge of the world, just to dump your body."
- Jarod Kintz

"She wasn't actually speaking to me, she was singing a kind of lullaby of talk. But, eventually, the music stopped. "
- Alice Sebold

"Music is closer to us, then; it streams toward us; we stand in its way, but then it goes right through us. It is almost like a higher air, we draw it into the lungs of spirit and it gives us a greater blood in the secret circulation."
- Rilke and Benventua

"Look, dude, you've sampled your life, mixed those sounds with a funk precedent, and established a sixteen-bar system of government for the entire rhythm nation. Set the Dj up as the executive, the legislative, and judicial branches. I mean, after listening to your beat, anything I've heard on the pop radio in the last five years feels like a violation of my civil rights."
- Paul Beatty

"If you were music
I would listen to you ceaselessly
 And my low spirits would brighten up."
- Anna Akhmatova

"We act out our lives to a soundtrack, thought Isabel, the music that becomes, for a spell, out favourite and is listened to again and again until it stands for the time itself. But that was about all the scripting that we achieved; the rest, for most of us, was extemporising."
- Alexander McCall Smith

"Play always as if in the presence of a master."
- Robert Schumann

"Music took her somewhere, and I used to wonder where. I thought it was dumb, the way she lived for a collection of sounds, for someone else's words and notes."

- Megan Lindholm

"If we are in a general way permitted to regard human activity in the realm of the beautiful as a liberation of the soul, as a release from constraint and restriction, in short to consider that art does actually alleviate the most overpowering and tragic catastrophes by means of the creations it offers to our contemplation and enjoyment, it is the art of music which conducts us to the final summit of that ascent to freedom."
- Georg Wilhelm Friedrich Hegel

"We are stardust? Billion-year old carbon, And we've got to get ourselves back to the garden"
- Joni Mitchell

"By the time the last few notes fade, his hope will be restored, but each time he's force to resort to the Adagio it becomes harder, and he knows its effect is finite. There are only a certain number of Adagios left in him, and he will not recklessly spend this precious currency. "
- Steven Galloway

"Jazz will endure as long as people hear it through their feet instead of their brains "
- John Philip Sousa

"When Johnson started singing, he seemed like a guy who could have sprung from the head of Zeus in full armor."
- Bob Dylan

"The aim and final end of all music should be none other than the glory of God and the refreshment of the soul."
- Johann Sebastian Bach

"One thing I like about jazz, kid, is that I don't know what's going to happen next. Do you?"
- Bix Beiderbecke

"Our musicians in residence carry this belief into the classroom. They don't think of children's self-esteem as so fragile that it will be shattered by the suggestion that the child guessed wrong or jumped to an invalid conclusion. They make corrections matter of factually, with no feeling that a child is a failure because she has made an error, but with confidence that the feedback will help the child learn and be accurate the next time."
- Peter Perret

"If I were to begin life again, I would devote it to music. It is the only cheap and unpunished rapture upon earth. "
- Sydney Smith

"Modern man is full of platitudes about living life to its fullest, with catchy key chain phrases and little plaques for kitchen walls. But if you've never retreated to the solitude of a dark room and listened to Beethoven's Ninth from start to finish, you know nothing. For music is a transcendental exploration of human emotion and experience, the very fabric of life in its purest form. And the Ninth our greatest musical achievement."
- Tiffany Madison

"As for the piano, the faster her fingers flew over it, the more he marveled. She struck the keys with aplomb and ran from one end of the keyboard to the other without a stop."
- Gustave Flaubert

"I won't look back to regret yesterday, we're not handed tomorrow so I'll live for today"
- 3 Doors Down

"Music is everything and nothing. It is useless and no limit can be set on its use. Music takes me to places of illimitable sensual and insensate joy, accessing points of ecstasy that no angelic lover could ever locate, or plunging me into gibbering weeping

hells of pain that no torturer could devise. Music makes me write this sort of maundering adolescent nonsense without embarrassment. Music is in fact the dog's bollocks. Nothing else comes close."
- Stephen Fry

"Music is everywhere. It's in the air between us, waiting to be sung."
- David Levithan

"It's not enough just to do those things anymore; what you must do instead if you want success on any large scale is either figure out a way of getting yourself associated in the audience's mind with their pities and their sense of 'community,' i.e. ram it home that you're one of THEM; or, alternately, deck and bake yourself into an image configuration so blatant or outrageous that you become a culture myth."
- Lester Bangs

"Music is what I have to do, I only answer the questions so that I can do it."
- Jack White

"Musical training is a more potent instrument than any other, because rhythm and harmony find their way into the inward places of the soul."
- Plato

"This is one of my favorite things about the Underground: the crashing of the cymbals, the screeching guitar riffs, music that moves into the blood and makes you feel hot and wild and alive."
- Lauren Oliver

"Want people to rock out in the car and not care that people are watching, I love that feeling when the sequences are all perfect

and you can just press play. I want the music to take you on a journey."
- Blake Lewis

"Hardcore without punk isn't music, it's a genre of porn. And punk isn't a genre of music, it's a thought process."
- Dominic Owen Mallary

"There is a music for lonely hearts nearly always.
If the music dies down there is a silence.
Almost the same as the movement of music.
To know silence perfectly is to know music."
- Carl Sandburg

"The Peruvian flute music is . . . cool. In this music, they have not yet invented the industrial revolution that leads to excessive punctuality or the failed experiment they call the nuclear family. This is the music of elements, untarnished, unrehearsed."
- Kate Braverman

"People usually complain that music is so ambiguous, and what they are supposed to think when they hear it is so unclear, while words are understood by everyone. But for me it is exactly the opposite...what the music I love expresses to me are thoughts not to indefinite for words, but rather too definite."
- Felix Mendelssohn

"Music, I think, he makes me feel like music."
- Lauren Oliver

"Music is a mixed mathematical science that concerns the origins, attributes, and distinctions of sound, out of which a cultivated and lovely melody and harmony are made, so that God is honored and praised but mankind is moved to devotion, virtue, joy, and sorrow."
- Christoph Wolff

"Music may be the activity that prepared our pre-human ancestors for speech communication and for the very cognitive, representational flexibility necessary to become humans."
- Daniel J. Levitin

"Always wear cute pajamas to bed, you'll never know who u will meet in your dreams."
- Joel Madden

"If heartache was a physical pain
I could face, I could face
But your hurting me from inside of my head
And I can't take it, I can't take it
I'm going to lose my mind"
- The Wanted

"Learning music by reading about it is like making love by mail."
- Luciano Pavarotti

"A kiss is a course of procedure cunningly devised, for the mutual stoppage of speech at a moment when words are superfluous."
- Oliver Herford

"I like great music, but who doesn't? Oh yeah, deaf people."
- Jarod Kintz

"The verse is supposed to get you hard so the chorus can suck you off."
- M. Thomas Gammarino

"Two people, two hands, and two songs, in this case "Big Shot" and "Bette Davis Eyes." The lyrics of the two songs provided no commentary, honest or ironic, on the proceedings. They were

merely there and always underfoot, the insistent gray muck that was pop culture. It stuck to our shoes and we tracked it through our lives."
- Colson Whitehead

"The trouble with modern music is that it's somewhat too intellectual...the brain has been working a little more than the bigger muscle underneath."
- Charles E. Ives

"Music itself was color-blind but the media and the radio stations segregate it based on their perceptions of the artists."
- Anthony Kiedis

"I've probably been spit on more than any person alive outside of, I would say, a member of the prison system."
- Iggy Pop

"Unbelievable," I said when it was done. And Brilliant and Audio crack and That one will be everyone's breakup song, and so on, because great is never good enough for the artists; they always want to know exactly what you mean and which nanosecond of the song you mean it about."
- Kelley Eskridge

"When she listened to songs that she loved on the radio, something stirred inside her. A liquid ache spread under her skin, and she walked out of the world like a witch."
- Arundhati Roy

"With a feeling of despondency so intense that it was almost pleasurable, he got out his guitar.
So this was to be his condition now. What was he but a fragment of broken churned-up humanity washed up on this faraway shore? This was where his journey had brought him....
There mus be a song in this..."

- Marina Lewycka

"The harp sounds at each passing breeze, but that does not mean
the tune is masterfully played."
- Jacqueline Carey

"Jobs had begun to drop acid by then, and he turned Brennan on
to it as well, in a wheat field just outside Sunnyvale. "It was
great," he recalled. "I had been listening to a lot of Bach. All of a
sudden the whole field was playing Bach. It was the most
wonderful feeling of my life up to that point. I felt like the
conductor of this symphony with Bach coming through the
wheat."
- Steve Jobs

"Writing about music is like dancing about architecture."
- Thelonious Monk

"I don't care if he hangs out with Skream/Benga or whoever," he
spat, "it's just pure nonsense to ruin a hardcore genre with gay
synths, chopped chipmunk vocals and cheesy poppy shit just so
you can make a shitload of money and be an icon to a fanbase
that consists of 13 year old wannabe dubheads and doesn't know
shit about music."
- Skrillex

"It is a well known fact that most artists produce their best work
early in their career. They may refine what they do but you
usually get the measure of what they are about on their first
outing."
- Bill Drummond

"There's something beautifully friendly and elevating about a
bunch of guys playing music together. This wonderful little
world that is unassailable. It's really teamwork, one guy
supporting the others, and it's all for one purpose, and there's no
flies in the ointment, for a while. And nobody conducting, it's all

up to you. It's really jazz__that's the big secret. Rock and roll ain't nothing but jazz with a hard backbeat."
- Keith Richards

"A bit of the vagueness of music stops you going completely mad, I imagine."
- Sebastian Faulks

"I'd sooner have died than admit that the most valuable thing I owned was a fairly extensive collection of German industrial music dance mix EP records stored for even further embarrassment under a box of crumbling Christmas tree ornaments in a Portland, Oregon basement. So I told him I owned nothing of any value."
- Douglas Coupland

"Art is why I get up in the morning, but my definition ends there. You know, it doesn't seem fair that I'm living for something I can't even define, but there you are, right there, in the meantime."
- Ani DiFranco

"Because all the brilliant ones- they can sing it and they can paint it, but they can't do it. You can't expect them to love you."
- Dakota Lane

"You will be most readily cured of vanity or presumption by studying the history of music, and by hearing the master pieces which have been produced at different periods."
- Robert Schumann

"The Who got paid 4000 pounds during those days, but we always smashed our equipment that cost more than 5000 pounds."
- Pete Townshend

"The radio is in the hands of such a lot of fools trying' to

anesthetize the way that you feel."
- Elvis Costello

"We have seen year after year the passion you have for music, and the way you have always been incredibly passionate fans, even though Hanson has not always been the coolest thing to be into."
- Hanson

"Learning to read music in Braille & play by ear helped me develop a very good memory."
- Ray Charles

"The music at a wedding procession always reminds me of the music of soldiers going into battle."
- Heinrich Heine

"Got to go sing in a few minutes... no, that's GOT to go sing in a few minutes, as in... GOT TO GO SING in a few minutes... hahaha It's an all consuming compassion/obsession... a drawing... a wonderful bliss... a union of soul and spirit, of notes and voice, of all of life's vibrating essence. String theory... all of life is vibrating, is alive, and the life of that essence is music itself!!"
- Gloria Smith

"So cry if you need to, but I can't stay to watch you. That's the wrong thing to do. Touch if you need to, but I can't stay to hold you. That's the wrong thing to do. Talk if you need to, but I can't stay to hear you. That's the wrong thing to do. Cause you say you love me, and I'll end up lying and say I love you too."
- Drake

"I just want to hear something I haven't heard before"
- John Peel

"Does not… the ear of Handel predict the witchcraft of harmonic sound?"
- Ralph Waldo Emerson

"If we can write or sing or create in some way, even when we are dealing with difficulties or pain, then it becomes something bigger than ourselves — and often beautiful."
- Brenda Peterson

"Toward the end, a band that had a young fellow from Philadelphia, Pennsylvania—I remember on account of him saying it two or three times and laughing every time that he did—played a song called 'All She Gets from the Iceman is Ice.' It made the grown folks, most of them anyway, howl laughing. I don't think I ever seen Mama laugh so hard. When it was about over, the sheriff come up and made them stop playing it, but he was grinning, too, so I figured he was just making them stop as part of the show."
- Eddie Whitlock

"That innate love of melody, which she had inherited from her ballad-singing mother, gave the simplest music a power which could well-nigh drag her heart out of her bosom at times."
- Thomas Hardy

"A digital sound sample in angry rap doesn't correspond to the graffiti but the wall."
- Jaron Lanier

"I was hungry when I left Pyongyang. I wasn't hungry just for a bookshop that sold books that weren't about Fat Man and Little Boy. I wasn't ravenous just for a newspaper that had no pictures of F.M. and L.B. I wasn't starving just for a TV program or a piece of music or theater or cinema that wasn't cultist and hero-worshiping. I was hungry. I got off the North Korean plane in Shenyang, one of the provincial capitals of Manchuria, and the

airport buffet looked like a cornucopia. I fell on the food, only to find that I couldn't do it justice, because my stomach had shrunk. And as a foreign tourist in North Korea, under the care of vigilant minders who wanted me to see only the best, I had enjoyed the finest fare available."
- Christopher Hitchens

"For the most basic assumption that dictated my early attempts to respond to creative music commentary was the mistaken belief that western journalists had some fundamental understanding of black creativity—or even western creativity—but this assumption was seriously in error."
- Anthony Braxton

"Music is a total constant. That's why we have such a strong visceral connection to it, you know? Because a song can take you back instantly to a moment, or a place, or even a person. No matter what else has changed in you or the world, that one song stays the same, just like that moment."
- Sarah Dessen

"A good song should life your heart, warm the soul and make you feel good."
- Colbie Caillat

"It is a great, a pleasant thing to have a friend with whom to walk, untroubled, through the woods, by the stream, saying nothing, at peace--the heart all clean and quiet and empty, ready for the spirit that may choose to be its guest."
- Catherine Drinker Bowen

"We speak in (rich) monotones. Our poetry is haunted by the music it has left behind. Orpheus shrinks to a poet when he looks back, with the impatience of reason, on a music stronger than death."
- George Steiner

"If, while at the piano, you attempt to form little melodies, that is very well; but if they come into your mind of themselves, when you are not practicing, you may be still more pleased; for the internal organ of music is then roused in you. The fingers must do what the head desires; not the contrary."
- Robert Schumann

"What is the purpose of writing music? One is, of course, not dealing with purposes but dealing with sounds. Or the answer must take the form of a paradox: a purposeful purposeless or a purposeless play. This play, however, is an affirmation of life-- not an attempt to bring order out of chaos nor to suggest improvements in creation, but simply a way of waking up to the very life we're living, which is so excellent once one gets one's mind and one's desires out of its way and lets it act of its own accord."
- John Cage

"As one old gentleman put it, " Son, I don't care if you're stark naked and wear a bone in your nose. If you kin fiddle, you're all right with me. It's the music we make that counts."
- Robert Fulghum

"You paid to see satire and rage. I swear I won't let Beauty set foot on this stage"
- Tim Minchin

"Life is waiting for you. It's all messed up but we're alive. Life is waiting for you. It's all messed up but we'll survive."
- Raine Maida

"Without enthusiasm nothing great can be effected in art."
- Robert Schumann

"Judge not lest ye be judged yourself."
- Metallica

"Now that rock is turning 50, it's become classical itself. It's interesting to see that development."
- Björk

"Rap has been a path between cultures in the best tradition of popular music."
- Jay-Z

"Noise has one advantage. It drowns out words. And suddenly he realized that all his life he had done nothing but talk, write, lecture, concoct sentences, search for formulations and amend them, so in the end no words were precise, their meanings were obliterated, their content lost, they turned into trash, chaff dust, sand; prowling through his brain, tearing at his head. they were his insomnia, his illness. And what he yearned for at that moment, vaguely, but with all his might, was unbounded music, absolute sound, a pleasant and happy all-encompassing, over powering, window-rattling din to engulf, once and for all, the pain, the futility, the vanity of words. Music was the negation of sentences, music was the anti-word!"
- Milan Kundera

"Wagner's music is better than it sounds"
- Mark Twain

"Then the bow orchestra began to play an apocalyptically beautiful canon, one of those pieces in which, surely, the composer simply transcribed what was given, and trembled in awe of the hand that was guiding him."
- Mark Helprin

"I started out with nothing and I've still got most of it left."
- Seasick Steve

"Charles laughingly observed,'Gospel and the blues are really, if you break it down, almost the same thing. It's just a question of whether you're talking' about a woman or God."
- Craig Werner

"Butterflies, butterflies
They were meant to fly
You and I, you and I
We were colors in the sky"
- The Wanted

"Hang my head, drown my fear, 'til you all just disappear."
- Soundgarden

"There's always that song that brings you back to the past. That makes you pause in the middle of what you're doing just so you could hear it clearly. The words bringing you back to a time that seemed nearly impossible, the words making you think for one moment that time itself has actually stopped. And there's nothing but you & perfect melody that brings you one step closer to what used to be."
- Kira Jeffries

"Music is very personal. It means different things to different people. To you it means belonging. To me it means knowing I exist."
- Simon Cheshire

"When all of this music sounds like you know what you want to say, then it will have been of all worth, ever. You will be something complete unto yourself, present and unique."
- Jeff Buckley

"The music brought us what it seemed / We had long desired, but in a form / so rarefied there was no emptiness of sensation"
- John Ashbery

"You could name practically any problem in the hood and there would be a rap song for you."
- Jay-Z

"I remembered that Beethoven's symphonies had sometimes been given names... they should have call [the Fifth] the Vampire, because it simply refused to lie down and die."
- Alan Bradley

"It bewildered Ig, the idea that a person could not be interested in music. It was like not being interested in happiness."
- Joe Hill

"The music never leaves. Once you have it, you can't lose it."
- Luanne Rice

"Its language is a language which the soul alone understands, but which the soul can never translate. "
- Arnold Bennett

"Our moments are music, and sometimes – just sometimes – we can catch them and put them into some lasting form. If we didn't have music, I don't think we could ever be truly happy, and if we didn't have special moments, we would never find music."
- David Levithan

"The kingdom of music is not the kingdom of this world; it will accept those whom breeding and intellect and culture have alike rejected."
- E.M. Forster

"It's asking for trouble to listen to music alone."
- Janice Galloway

"If it is art, it is not for all, and if it is for all, it is not art."
- Arnold Schoenberg

"Big fat hairy monkey, hands a couple of octaves wide?"
- Terry Pratchett

"A musician's or artist's responsibility is a simple one, and that is, through your music to tell the truth,"
- Tom Morello

"It was like being at an Arabian hoedown with a band of psychedelic hillbillies."
- Patti Smith

"The music lets me see the story but the story doesn't let me write the words."
- Elizabeth J. Kolodziej

"What can a man do with music who is not benevolent?"
- Confucius

"Music without the ebb and flow would be like "watching a film with only good guys in it."
- John Powell

"Music is the heart of life." She speaks love; "without it, there is no possible good and with it everything is beautiful."
- Franz Liszt

"Led Zep played with light and shade, ear-splitting noise and echoing quiet. They could do it all."
- Quinton Skinner

"Without music life would B flat"
- Dulcinea Martinez

"The sound of the king's music made Despereaux's soul grow large and light inside of him."
- Kate DiCamillo

"How can you understand the language of music, if you will not be an instrument
- Greg Hamerton

"I've never heard of anybody getting rid of their prized Exile postcards, much less actually writing on them and sending them through the mail to a girl. I watched these two, laughing over this story at the same kitchen table they've shared for thirty years. I realize that I will never fully understand the millions of bizarre ways that music brings people together."
- Rob Sheffield

"I was no longer able to hear the music that issues from a decent piece of prose."
- Carlos Ruiz Zafón

"I have no doubt that, had I actually been growing up in the 1930s or 1940s, I would have been grooving to turn-of-the-century beats."
- Emma Brockes

"A quiet secluded life in the country, with the possibility of being useful to people to whom it is easy to do good… then work which one hopes may be of some use; then rest, nature, books, music, love for one's neighbor? such is my idea of happiness."
- Leo Tolstoy

"On the Rolling Stones - You will walk out of the Amphitheater after watching the Stones perform and suddenly the Chicago stockyards smell clean and good by comparison."
- Tom Fitzpatrick

"Music is a holy place, a cathedral so majestic that we can sense the magnificence of the universe."
- Don Campbell

"The chanting went on, the musicians giving in to the rhythm of their own being, finding healing in touching that rhythm, and healing in chanting about death, the only real god they knew."
- Karl Marlantes

"Often the right path is the one that may be hardest for you to follow. But the hard path is also the one that will make you grow as a human being."
- Karen Mueller Coombs

"When I bestride him, I soar. I am a hawk: he trots the air. The earth sings when he touches it; the basest horn of his hoof is more musical than the pipe of Hermes."
- William Shakespeare

"I think there is a song out there to describe just about any situation."
- Criss Jami

"Where is the line? Where is the line?
To be your self is not a crime"
- Billy Talent

"Don't worry about the future, sooner or later it's the past. If they say the feeling's gone then it's time to take it back."
- Meat Loaf

"Some have muses to inspire them. I have music."
- Maysa Costa de Araujo

"All we shared was a mattress, and a lie, and an address.

Baby I don't need you, well baby I don't need you.
Once occupied by a goddess, now it's a room full of boxes.
She said, "it's time to leave you" but baby I don't need you!
In a perfect world... her face would not exist.
In a perfect world... a broken heart is fixed"
- Billy Talent

"The deaf people there with balloons, holding them up and
feeling the vibrations of the balloons to the Germs, all these
f******' great bands, and using these balloons and dancing
around. For a tough old punk, it just made your heart -- it gave
you that beautiful feeling. They loved the music, and we were
making money for them."
- Jack Boulware

"If anybody can appreciate fine music, it's me. I mean who else
can hit multiple octaves with their armpits?"
- Jarod Kintz

"White folks have controlled New Orleans with money and
guns, black folks have controlled it with magic and music, and
although there has been a steady undercurrent of mutual
admiration, an intermingling of cultures unheard of in any other
American city, South or North; although there has prevailed a
most joyous and fascinating interface, black anger and white fear
has persisted, providing the ongoing, ostensibly integrated fete
champeter with volatile and sometimes violent idiosyncrasies."
- Tom Robbins

"The air was warm and heavy as sprinkles began to fall from the
clouds high above. The Triton glided through the waters and the
whoosh of the ship combined with the steady beat of the rain to
make a concerto, like a pianist fluttering his fingers on the keys
at one end and running his fingers up and down the scales at the
other. Expectancy hung in the air as the tune moved to a
crescendo."

- Victoria Kahler

"You can go a hundred miles a second
Don't have to drive no lousy cab
Got everything you want and more man
And the King picks up the tab
You walk around on streets of gold all day
And you never have to listen
To what these customers say and I know..."
- Marc Cohn

"They're events you remember all your life, like your first real orgasm. And the whole purpose of the absurd, mechanically persistent involvement with recorded music is the pursuit of that priceless moment. So it's not exactly that records might unhinge the mind, but rather that if anything is going to drive you up the wall it might as well be a record."
- Lester Bangs

"Or maybe memories are like karaoke - where you realize up on the stage, with all those lyrics scrawling across the screen's bottom, and with everybody clapping at you, that you didn't even know the lyrics to your all-time favorite song. Only afterward's, when someone else is up on stage humiliating themselves amid the clapping and laughing, do you realize that what you liked most about your favorite song was precisely your ignorance of its full meaning - and you read more into it than maybe existed in the first place. I think it's better not to know the lyrics to your life."
- Douglas Coupland

"Musicians add to songs and they evolve: For as was true of human effort, there was never advancement. Everything added meant something lost, and about as often as not the thing lost was preferable to the thing gained, so that over time we'd be lucky if we just broke even. Any thought otherwise was empty pride."

- Charles Frazier

"There is simply no limit to the tyrannical snobbery that otherwise decent people can descend into when it comes to music."
- Stephen Fry

"A good compilation tape, like breaking up, is hard to do. You've got to kick off with a corker, to hold the attention (I started with 'Got To Get You Off My Mind', but then realized that she might not get any further than track one, side one if I delivered what she wanted straight away, so I buried it in the middle of side two), and then you've got to up it a notch, and you can't have white music and black music together, unless the white music sounds like black music, and you can't have two tracks by the same artist side by side, unless you've done the whole thing in pairs, and ... oh there are loads of rules."
- Nick Hornby

"Nothing is accomplished by writing a piece of music
nothing is accomplished by hearing a piece of music
nothing is accomplished by playing a piece of music
our ears are now in excellent condition."
- John Cage

"Every time you go in, it's like starting over. You don't know how you did the other records. You're learning all over. It's some weird musician amnesia, or maybe the road wipes it out."
- Beck

"I cringed as the band oozed into the next chord. If notes were cars, I think there was a D major under the wreckage."
- Mary Hughes

"Color is the keyboard, the eyes are the harmonies, the soul is the piano with many strings. The artist is the hand that plays, touching one key or another, to cause vibrations in the soul."

- Wassilly Kandinsky

"For a short while she considered the idea of orchestral courtesy. Certainly one should avoid giving political offense: German orchestras, of course, used to be careful about playing Wagner abroad, at least in some countries, choosing instead German composers who were somewhat more ... apologetic."
- Alexander McCall Smith

"Spent the fortnight gone in the music room reworking my year's fragments into a 'sextet for overlapping soloists': piano, clarinet, 'cello, flute, oboe, and violin, each in its own language of key, scale, and color. In the first set, each solo is interrupted by its successor; in the second, each interruption is re-continued, in order. Revolutionary or gimmicky? Shan't know until it's finished, and by then it'll be too late."
- David Mitchell

"Notes and chords have become my second language and, more often than not, that vocabulary expresses what I feel when language fails me. The guitar is my conscience, too - whenever I've lost my way, it's brought me back to center; whenever I forget, it reminds me why I'm here."
- Slash

"Gloria watched the swollen white orb of a hot-air balloon rising over Navy Pier and knew she had to break it off with Oliver, for he was the type who would never enjoy hot-air balloons, Van Morrison songs, or mess, whether from orgasm or otherwise. But who was she to be dreaming about mess today?"
- Andrea Kayne Kaufman

"TV taught me how to feel. Now real life has no appeal."
- Marina and the Diamonds

"Culture's just a bore, when your angry, young & poor."
- The Damned

"I'd spend hours in HMVs, Virgin Megastores and second-hand record shops staffed by greasy-haired 40-year-olds dressed as 20-year-olds, listening to contemporary music of every genre – Britrock, heavy maiden, gang rap, brake beat. And I came to a startling but unshakeable conclusion: no genuinely good music has been created since 1988."
- Alan Partridge

"He was waiting for me at the best table in the room, toying with a glass of white wine and listening to the pianist who was playing a piece by Granados with velvet fingers."
- Carlos Ruiz Zafón

"We're not into music. We're into chaos."
- Steve Jones

"I was never very good with either my hands or feet. It always seemed to me they'd just been stuck on as an afterthought during my making. Dreams didn't translate through sports, or music, dancing, carpentry, plumbing. I was the bookish kid, more at home in the pages of a fantasy than in the room in the town on the planet."
- Steve Rasnic Tem

"Rosa Parks sat so Martin Luther King could walk. Martin Luther King walked so Obama could run. Obama's running so we all can fly."
- Jay-Z

"Bring wings to the weak and bring grace to the strong
May all evil stumble as it flies in the world
All the tribes comes and the mighty will crumble
We must brave this night and have faith in love"
- Janelle Monáe

"I have my own particular sorrows, loves, delights; and you have yours. But sorrow, gladness, yearning, hope, love, belong to all of us, in all times and in all places. Music is the only means whereby we feel these emotions in their universality."
- Overstreet

"Think it a vile habit to alter works of good composers, to omit parts of them, or to insert new-fashioned ornaments. This is the greatest insult you can offer to Art."
- Robert Schumann

"It's easy to play any musical instrument: all you have to do is touch the right key at the right time and the instrument will play itself."
- Johann Sebastian Bach

"If we are exhorted to play simple melodies with beauty rather than difficult ones with error, the same should be applied to writing; simple words greater effect."
- Sonia Rumzi

"My first kiss. A new kind of kiss, like the new kind of music still playing, softly, in the distance - wild and arrhythmic, desperate. Passionate."
- Lauren Oliver

"As Steve draws me closer to the band, all I can see is a frenzied mass of seething, writhing people, like a many-headed sea snake, grinding, waving their arms, stamping their feet, jumping. No rules, just energy - so much energy, you could harness it; I bet you could power Portland for a decade. It is more than a wave. It's a tide, an ocean of bodies."
- Lauren Oliver

"The power of music, whether joyous or cathartic must steal on one unawares, come spontaneously as a blessing or a grace--"

- Oliver Sacks

"Disco's are tricky. You look a total wally if you dance too early but after one crucial song tips the disco over, you look a sad if you don't."
- David Mitchell

"We're deaf men working as musicians; we play the music but we can't hear it."
- Sebastian Faulks

"He went on to tell her that certain work songs made the work a little easier, but that there were others, depending upon the time of day, that dragged a body down, so 'you just gotta be careful with your songs and your humming' and whatnot."
- Edward P. Jones

"My friend Kate once went to a concert of Mongolian throat singers who were traveling through New York City on a rare world tour. Although she couldn't understand the words to their songs, she found the music almost unbearably sad. After the concert, Kate approached the lead Mongolian singer and asked, "What are your songs about?" He replied, "Our songs are about the same things that everyone else's songs are about: lost love, and somebody stole your fastest horse."
- Elizabeth Gilbert

"Pianos, unlike people, sing when you give them your every growl. They know how to dive into the pit of your stomach and harmonize with your roars when you've split yourself open. And when they see you, guts shining, brain pulsing, heart right there exposed in a rhythm that beats need need, need need, need need, pianos do not run. And so she plays."
- Francesca Lia Block

"I could have been a famous singer, if I had someone else's voice."
- Conor Oberst

"The only thing--I tell you this straight from the heart--that disgusts me in Salzburg is that one can't have any proper social intercourse with those people--and that music does not have a better reputation...For I assure you, without travel, at least for people from the arts and sciences, one is a miserable creature!...A man of mediocre talents always remains mediocre, may he travel or not--but a man of superior talents, which I cannot deny myself to have without being blasphemous, becomes--bad, if he always stays in the same place. If the archbishop would trust me, I would soon make his music famous; that is surely true."
- Wolfgang Amadeus Mozart

"In scientific thinking are always present elements of poetry. Science and music requires a thought homogeneous."
- Albert Einstein

"My first kiss. A new kind of kiss, like the new kind of music still playing, softly, in the distance - wild and arrhythmic, desperate. Passionate."
- Lauren Oliver

"There is no pattern the human mind can devise that does not exist already within the bounds of nature...Everything we do, see, write, notate, all are an echo of the deep seams of the universe. Music is the invisible world made visible through sound."
- Kate Mosse

"Music straightjackets a poem and prevents it from breathing on its own, whereas it liberates a lyric. Poetry doesn't need music; lyrics do."
- Stephen Sondheim

"So imagine that the lovely moon is playing just for you - everything makes music if you really want it to."
- Giles Andreae

"There are, of course, inherent tendencies to repetition in music itself. Our poetry, our ballads, our songs are full of repetition; nursery rhymes and the little chants and songs we use to teach young children have choruses and refrains. We are attracted to repetition, even as adults; we want the stimulus and the reward again and again, and in music we get it. Perhaps, therefore, we should not be surprised, should not complain if the balance sometimes shifts too far and our musical sensitivity becomes a vulnerability."
- Oliver Sacks

"Partying means drinking. It also means playing records by Lou Reed and Chicago, which I thought was a city but is also a band it turns out."
- Ron Currie Jr.

"When I'm on stage, I'm trying to do one thing: bring people joy. Just like church does. People don't go to church to find trouble, they go there to lose it."
- James Brown

"Literature is painting, architecture, and music."
- Yevgeny Zamyatin

"And then I notice the music flooding out of every part of the apartment at once the couch, the walls, even the floor, and I know Bennies alone in Lou's studio, pouring music down around us. A minute ago it was "Don't Let Me Down". Then it was Blondie's "Heart of Glass". Now it's Iggy Pop's "The Passenger". Listening, I think, You will never know how much I understand you."
- Jennifer Egan

"Choice betrays character," I said.

"That's not true." Loring moved his finger along the sheet as if writing his name in cursive. "Eliza, you can't judge a man solely on his actions. Sometimes actions are nothing more than reactions."
- Tiffany Debartolo

"From time to time, too, and for the space of two or three paces, an image or an echo would rise up from the recesses of time: in the little streets of the beaters of silver and gold, for instance, there was a clear, unhurried tinkling, as if a djinn with a thousand arms was absent-mindedly practising on a xylophone."
- Claude Lévi-Strauss

"Like punk rock, like Jackson Pollock, like Jack Kerouac, it was truly human, a mix of perfect beauty and cathartic error."
- Yann Martel

"There's never a dull day,
When you're beaten by nonfiction."
- Jay Farrar

"I think that is what film and art and music do; they can work as a map of sorts for your feelings."
- Bruce Springsteen

"The way I choose to show my feelings is through my songs."
- Marianne Faithfull

"Pianos, unlike people, sing when you give them your every growl. They know how to dive into the pit of your stomach and harmonize with your roars when you've split yourself open. And when they see you, guts shining, brain pulsing, heart right there exposed in a rhythm that beats need need, need need, need need, pianos do not run. And so she plays."
- Francesca Lia Block

"I think there's no greater joy than completing a song out of thin air. It's like inventing something, but it's invisible, you know? It's weird. It amazes me. You can send it out in the world, and that's the joy. It's like giving birth to all these songs and letting them go like they're your kids."
- Jason Mraz

"It was a full Spears album, apparently, and each song was as ridiculous as the one before. They were catchy, yes, but so was the plague."
- Heidi Cullinan

"I listen'd, motionless and still;
And, as I mounted up the hill,
The music in my heart I bore,
Long after it was heard no more."
- William Wordsworth

"I'm so cool that the kids come to my bedroom and go, 'Mom! Turn the music down!"
- Melissa Etheridge

"I do not like the raw sound of the human voice in unison unless it is under the discipline of music."
- Flannery O'Connor

"And all meet in singing, which braids together the different knowings into a wide and subtle music, the music of living. "
- Alison Croggon

"With the world's fate resting on your shoulder - you're gonna need someone on your side.
You can't do it by yourself any longer - you're gonna need someone on your side."
- Morrissey

"In the end we're all just chalk lines on the concrete
Drawn only to be washed away
For the time that I've been given
I am what I am"
- Five Finger Death Punch

"But the Beast was a good person...the Prince looked on the outside the way the Beast was on the inside. Sometimes people couldn't see the inside of the person unless they like the outside of a person. Because they hadn't learned to hear the music yet."
- Karen Kingsbury

"One thing he discovered with a great deal of astonishment was that music held for him more then just pleasure. There was meat to it. The grouping of sounds, their forms in the air as they rang out and faded, said something comforting to him about the rule of Creation. What the music said was that there is a right way for things to be ordered so that life might not always be just tangle and drift, but have a shape, an aim. It was a powerful argument that life did not just happen."
- Charles Frazier

"Musically, he was like an old man in a boy's skin."
- Eric Clapton

"My music is the spiritual expression of what I am — my faith, my knowledge, my being...When you begin to see the possibilities of music, you desire to do something really good for people, to help humanity free itself from its hangups...I want to speak to their souls."
- John Coltrane

"Lord, I feel so small sometimes in this great big old world.
Yeah, I know there are more important things.
But don't forget to remember me."
- Carrie Underwood

"If you play "I Don't Want To Know" by Fleetwood Mac loud enough -- you can hear Lindsey Buckingham's fingers sliding down the strings of his acoustic guitar. ...And we were convinced that this was the definitive illustration of what we both loved about music; we loved hearing the INSIDE of a song."
- Chuck Klosterman

"Music is not take it or leave it; Music is life or death!"
- Joss Stirling

"Mr. Mancini had a singular talent for making me uncomfortable. He forced me to consider things I'd rather not think about – the sex of my guitar, for instance. If I honestly wanted to put my hands on a woman, would that automatically mean I could play? Gretchen's teacher never told her to think of her piano as a boy. Neither did Lisa's flute teacher, though in that case the analogy was obvious. On the off chance that sexual desire was all it took, I steered clear of Lisa's instrument, fearing that I might be labeled a prodigy."
- David Sedaris

"I turned to the clarinets. They were a resourceful lot."
- Jennifer Echols

"I think music is what language once aspired to be. Music allows us to face God on our own terms because it reaches beyond life."
- Simon Van Booy

"At first the music almost repelled me, it was so intense, and this man made no attempt to sugarcoat what he was trying to say, or play. It was hard-core, more than anything I had ever heard. After a few listenings I realized that, on some level, I had found the master, and that following this man's example would be my life's work."
- Eric Clapton

"I tell you such fine music waits in the shadows of Hell."
- Charles Bukowski

"Music defines us, for it shapes our souls and minds."
- Jessica Carroll

"In the brightest hour of my darkest day, I realized what is wrong with me" ~Forever"
- Papa Roach

"People are strange when you're a stranger."
- Jim Morrison

"There's a friendly tie of some sort between music and eating."
- Thomas Hardy

"If you understand or if you don't
If you believe or if you doubt
There's a universal justice
And the eyes of truth
Are always watching you"
- Enigma

"Dance with the Devil"
- Breaking Benjamin

"There are two kinds of artists left: those who endorse Pepsi and those who simply won't."
- Annie Lennox

"I want to drum up interest for instruments that are played by beating them with sticks. "
- Jarod Kintz

"If you have to ask what jazz is, you'll never know."
- Louis Armstrong

"There are more than enough to fight and oppose;
why waste good time fighting the people you like?"
- Morrissey

"Music is forever; music should grow and mature with you,
following you right on up until you die. "
- Paul Simon

"Lie awake in bed at night and think about your life do you want
to be different?"
- 30 Seconds to Mars

"Mostly all I have to say about these songs is that I love them,
and want to sing along to them, and force other people to listen
to them, and get cross when these other people don't like them as
much as I do. "
- Nick Hornby

"This world, I am afraid, is designed for crashing bores."
- Morrissey

"The first mistake of art is to assume that it's serious."
- Lester Bangs

"You can turn off the sun, but im still ganna shine!"
- Jason Mraz

"You don't have to have money, To make it in this world"
- Mcfly

"Good music always defeats bad luck"
- Jack Vance

"In music the passions enjoy themselves."
- Friedrich Nietzsche

"I can play the trumpet, but only if I have a sufficient quantity of anal lube."
- Jarod Kintz

"I have forgiven Jesus for all of the love he placed in me, when there's no one I can turn to with this love."
- Morrissey

"The large print giveth and the small print taketh away."
- Tom Waits

"Fashion and music are the same, because music express its period too."
- Karl Lagerfeld

"If you're going to play it out of tune, then play it out of tune properly."
- Mark E. Smith

"They all trying to say something with music that you can't say with plain talk. There ain't really no words for love or pain. And the way I see it, only fools go around trying to talk their love or talk their pain. So the smart people make music and you can kinda hear about it without them saying anything."
- Gloria Naylor

"Songwriters write songs, but they really belong to the listener."
- Jimmy Buffett

"Music can elevate man to new heights. Especially elevator music."
- Jarod Kintz

"Without music, life would be a mistake."
- Friedrich Nietzsche

"There are some bad people on the rise;
they're saving their own skins by ruining people's lives."
- Morrissey

"Music has power to create a universe or to destroy a
civilization."
- Katherine Neville

"There's a club, if you'd like to go
You could meet somebody who really loves you.'
So you go, and you stand on your own
And you leave on your own
And you go home, and you cry
And you want to die."
- Morrissey

"I'll be the one to protect you from your enemies and all your
demons.
I'll be the one to protect you from a will to survive and a voice of
reason.
I'll be the one to protect you from your enemies and your
choices, son.
They're one in the same, I must isolate you
Isolate and save you from yourself."
- A Perfect Circle

"He made me peppermint tea and I told him how he had ruined
every song on the tape for me, since now they all made me cry.
He corrected me, telling me that he had actually vitalized them
for me by infusing them with meaning. Maybe he was right. "
- Daniella Meeker

"To him the stars seemed like so many musical notes affixed to
the sky, just waiting for somebody to unfasten them. Someday
the sky would be emptied, but by then the earth would be a
constellation of musical scores"
- Machado de Assis

"Music is well said to be the speech of angels; in fact, nothing among the utterances allowed to man is felt to be so divine. It brings us near to the infinite."
- Thomas Carlyle

"God, come down, if you're really there -
Well, you're the one who claims to care!"
- Morrissey

"I could never be your God
And I don't even think I want the job anymore"
- Stone Sour

"A song nobody likes is a sad thing. But a love song nobody likes is hardly a thing at all."
- Rob Sheffield

"If one plays good music, people don't listen, and if one plays bad music people don't talk."
- Oscar Wilde

"You are the sun, and I'm the moon. In your shadow I can shine."
- Tokio Hotel

"Music expresses feeling and thought, without language; it was below and before speech, and it is above and beyond all words. "
- Robert G. Ingersoll

"After playing Chopin, I feel as if I had been weeping over sins that I had never committed, and mourning over tragedies that were not my own. Music always seems to me to produce that effect. It creates for one a past of which one has been ignorant, and fills one with a sense of sorrows that have been hidden from one's tears."

- Oscar Wilde

"What if I wanted to break, laugh it all off in your face, what would you do? What if I fell to the floor, couldn't take this anymore? What would you do??"
- 30 Seconds to Mars

"Philosophy is the highest music."
- Plato

"You know what punk is? a bunch of no-talent guys who really, really want to be in a band. Nobody reads music, nobody plays the mandolin, and you're too dumb to write songs about mythology or Middle-earth. So what's your style? Three chords, cranked out fast and loud and distorted because your instruments are crap and you can't play them worth a damn. And you scream your lungs out to cover up the fact that you can't sing. It should suck, but here's the thing - it doesn't. Rock and roll can be so full of itself, but not this. It's simple and angry and raw."
- Gordon Korman

"There is in souls a sympathy with sounds:
And as the mind is pitched the ear is pleased
With melting airs, or martial, brisk or grave;
Some chord in unison with what we hear
Is touched within us, and the heart replies."
- William Cowper

"On that same tour we ran into a band at Aylesbury Friars, a biggish venue in Oxfordshire, England. They were a four-piece from Ireland called U2. They seemed like nice fellows and they sounded pretty good, but we didn't keep in touch. They're probably taxi drivers and accountants by now."
- Craig Ferguson

"I'm not the one who's so far away
When I feel the snake bite enter my veins.

46

Never did I wanna be here again,
And I don't remember why I came."
- Sully Erna

"Mockingbirds are the true artists of the bird kingdom."
- Tom Robbins

"You fondle my trigger, then you blame my gun"
- Fiona Apple

"Rehearsals and practice times by myself are like these little islands of 'Okay' in a vast sea of 'Holy Crap!'"
- Jordan Sonnenblick

"The movies, I thought, have got the soundtrack to war all wrong. War isn't rock 'n' roll. It's got nothing to do with Jimi Hendrix or Richard Wagner. War is nursery rhymes and early Madonna tracks. War is the music from your childhood. Because war, when it's not making you kill or be killed, turns you into an infant. For the past eight days, I'd been living like a five-year-old , a nonexistence of daytime naps, mushy food, and lavatory breaks. My adult life was back in Los Angeles with my dirty dishes and credit card bills."
- Chris Ayres

"Music is nothing else but wild sounds civilized into time and tune."
- Thomas Fuller

""The sound of a barrel organ rising from the deepest golden vein of the day; two or three bars of a chorus, played on a distant piano over and over again, melting in the sun on the white pavement, lost in the fire of high noon."
- Bruno Schulz

"If one should desire to know whether a kingdom is well governed, if its morals are good or bad, the quality of its music will furnish the answer."
- Confucius

"Even now - in the final hour of my life - I'm falling in love again."
- Morrissey

"This is how it works. You're young until you're not. You love until you don't. You try until you can't. You laugh until you cry. You cry until you laugh. And everyone must breathe until their dying breath."
- Regina Spektor

"The ribbon on my wrist says: Do not open before Christmas."
- Fall Out Boy

"Talk about a dream, try to make it real"
- Bruce Springsteen

"One good thing about music, when it hits you, you feel no pain."
- Bob Marley

"You've got that smile,
That only heaven can make.
I pray to God everyday,
That you keep that smile.
Yeah, you are my dream,
There's not a thing I won't do.
I'd give my life up for you,
'Cause you are my dream."
- Chris Brown

"There is nothing more to be said or to be done tonight, so hand me over my violin and let us try to forget for half an hour the

miserable weather and the still more miserable ways of our fellowmen."
- Arthur Conan Doyle

"An intellectual snob is someone who can listen to the William Tell Overture and not think of The Lone Ranger. "
- Dan Rather

"What's even worse than a flute? - Two flutes!"
- Wolfgang Amadeus Mozart

"A poet's mission is to make words do more work than they normally do, to make them work on more than one level."
- Jay-Z

"Best friends just don't leave your side"
- Blink-182

"The truth is, going against the internal stream of ignorance is way more rebellious than trying to start some sort of cultural revolution."
- Noah Levine

"The sky is full of dreams, but you don't know how to fly."
- The Killers

"I think I should have no other mortal wants, if I could always have plenty of music. It seems to infuse strength into my limbs and ideas into my brain. Life seems to go on without effort, when I am filled with music."
- George Eliot

"Don't make it new; make it whole."
- Alex Ross

"Music is much like fucking, but some composers can't climax and others climax too often, leaving themselves and

the listener jaded and spent"
- Charles Bukowski

"To me, making a tape is like writing a letter – there's a lot of
erasing and rethinking and starting again, and I wanted it to be a
good one."
- Nick Hornby

"Our biological rhythms are the symphony of the cosmos, music
embedded deep within us to which we dance, even when we
can't name the tune."
- Deepak Chopra

"The world is teeming; anything can happen."
- John Cage

"The Only Way Out Is To DIE!!!!"
- Bullet for My Valentine

"Music is enough for a lifetime, but a lifetime is not enough for
music"
- Sergei Rachmaninov

"They said they respect me, which means, their judgment is
crazy."
- Morrissey

"Inspiration may be a form of super-consciousness, or
perhaps of subconsciousness—I wouldn't know. But I am
sure it is the antithesis of self-consciousness."
- Aaron Copland

"There's that thing that can happen to you when you meet
somebody and you don't consider them extraordinary at all and
then they do something like play the cello or write amazing
poetry or sing and suddenly you look at them completely
differently."

- Yvonne Prinz

"We didn't start the fire.
It was always burning.
Since the world's been turning.
We didn't start the fire.
No we didn't light it.
But we tried to fight it."
- Billy Joel

"God has abandoned you. Fear does not serve you. Your heart
has betrayed you. Only the music can guide you."
- Noah Levine

"The unhappiest people I know, romantically speaking, are the
ones who like pop music the most; and I don't know whether pop
music has caused this unhappiness, but I do know that they've
been listening to the sad songs longer than they've been living
the unhappy lives."
- Nick Hornby

"I love music. For me, music is morning coffee. It's mood
medicine. It's pure magic. A good song is like a good meal-I just
want to inhale it and then share a bite with someone else."
- Hoda Kotb

"Robert Kapilow is a born teacher, an enthusiast who can think
on his feet, a 110 percent believer in the project at hand ... It's a
cheering thought that this kind of missionary enterprise did not
pass from this earth with Leonard Bernstein. Robert Kapilow is
awfully good at what he does. We need him."
- Boston Globe

"You make me sick. Because I adore you so..."
~Space Dementia"
- Matthew J. Bellamy

"It reset and mended my freshly damaged and distorted view of life, and made me recognize that this thing we call music, this primal expression that we reshape and refine and define ourselves with, is the gift I was given. The ability to communicate what others feel but cannot fully express, the passing down and around of songs and stories, from Pete Townshend to Joey Ramone to me, to the audiences who take the time and effort to support our work and give us a way to support ourselves -- I'm thinking this is what I am supposed to be doing."
- Bob Mould

"I suppose what I mean is, I never felt like I was part of a gang. No, that's the wrong word. Part of a MOVEMENT! That's it. It feels like there's a swirling, shining wind of change sweeping right at you, sweeping over everyone, and you're inside it. It feels like there is something that transcends you, that goes beyond whatever you are, that is great and whole and good. Great, because when it all comes together it's so much more than all its individual pieces. Whole because you're part of it and if you weren't, then both you and it would be diminished. Good because at its core is pure talent and skill, like you know you'll never have yourself."
- Simon Cheshire

"I've never known a musician who regretted being one. Whatever deceptions life may have in store for you, music itself is not going to let you down."
- Virgil Thomson

"Songwriting is a bitch. And then it has puppies"
- Steven Tyler

"Love is friendship set to music"
- Erich W. Pollak

"We throw stones though we live in glass houses,
We talk shit like its a cross to bare.
You're only relevant 'til you get older.
Keep your friends close, and your enemies closer"
- Alex Gaskarth

"I think records were just a little bubble through time and those who made a living from them for a while were lucky. There is no reason why anyone should have made so much money from selling records except that everything was right for this period of time. I always knew it would run out sooner or later. It couldn't last, and now it's running out. I don't particularly care that it is and like the way things are going. The record age was just a blip. It was a bit like if you had a source of whale blubber in the 1840s and it could be used as fuel. Before gas came along, if you traded in whale blubber, you were the richest man on Earth. Then gas came along and you'd be stuck with your whale blubber. Sorry mate – history's moving along. Recorded music equals whale blubber. Eventually, something else will replace it."
- Brian Eno

"The powerful chords that emanated from the radio heated me from the inside out, like a microwave."
- Sandy Ward Bell

"All Townshend cared about was the music." The music industry could use more people like Pete Townshend who are concerned with good songs, not just good demographics. He has been making sure the kids are all right since you were in diapers, but he never manipulated them."
- Patrick Marsh

"There's no equivalent to Mozart in writing."
- Fran Lebowitz

"You can't be like pop stars, but you can be part of their story. You can be their fan."
- Simon Cheshire

"I believe that music is connected by human passions and curiosities rather than by marketing strategies."
- Elvis Costello

"When the music changes, so does the dance."
- African Proverb

"The way I played music there was the way I wanted to farm, chop wood, cook, make love, raise children. Everything. A lo of it had to do with things I felt while I played. If only I could feel that sense of total absorption in what I was doing when I was doing other things. It was more than absorption, it was spontaneity, competence, a sense of grace and playfulness, of being in touch with an inexhaustible source of energy and beauty."
- Mark Vonnegut

"We needed germans in Paris to hear Wagner."
- Marcel Proust

"Out of the choked Devonian waters emerged sight and sound and the music that rolls invisible through the composer's brain. They are there still in the ooze along the tideline, though no one notices. The world is fixed, we say: fish in the sea, birds in the air. But in the mangrove swamps by the Niger, fish climb trees and ogle uneasy naturalists who try unsuccessfully to chase them back to the water. There are things still coming ashore. "
- Loren Eiseley

"Music evokes emotion and emotion can bring it memory."
- Oliver Sacks

"On the boardwalk the arcade jukebox plays all night surrounded by teenagers--sometimes twenty bodies deep, bare-skinned and full of energy for the music, for one another, for life, for the little bit of freedom they taste in the salt air and their skin. My father finds his place in this crowd. They are a force together. They don't do drugs. They don't drink. But they do music, and their power comes from their numbers and the thrill of being young on the beach at night."
- Laura Schenone

"The music of revelation announces itself to the reader in somber brooding tones or in melodies light as air and one is invited to dance with the most captivating of partners: poetry."
- Aberjhani

"All these years the people said 'He's acting like a kid.' He did not know he could not fly, so he did. Well he's one of those that knows that life is just a leap of faith. So spread your arms, hold your breath and always trust your cape."Holy shit was this song bad. It was like the singer was
- Guy Clark

"Holy shit was this song bad. It was like the singer was stabbing my ear with a dagger made of dried turds."
- David Wong

"We all fall sometime, you're not the first. I know it hurts. In the end, you'll find what you deserve."
- Alter Bridge

"The boy Prewitt loved the songs because they gave him something, a first hint that pain might not be pointless if you could only turn it into something."
- James Jones

"You know when I'm down to my socks it's time for business

That's why they're called business socks
It's business, it's business time"
- Flight of the Conchords

"Accusing us of being a gimmick is a bit like accusing Jesus
Christ of having 'a bit of a messiah complex'. True, maybe, but
when faced with the undeniable genius of what we put out, does
that really still matter?"
- Gorillaz

"He knows how to market himself well. Nowadays, that's all that
seems to count. He's rebellious in a way that appeals to people
with vain, shallow taste. So of course he manipulates his
audiences with the blessing of his recording company and the
financial investors behind his brand."
- Jess C. Scott

"They [the critics] deal with Schoenberg's early works and all
their wealth by classifying them, with the music-historical
cliché, as late romantic post-Wagnerian. One might just as well
dispose of Beethoven as a late-classicist post-Haydnerian."
- Theodor W. Adorno

"There'll be no more music, Father. But there'll be this!" He
stepped into the dark, picked up the knife, and held it under their
noses.
"Go home. Tell your people what you saw and heard here
tonight. And tell 'em that anyone we catch on these roads after
dark anymore... this is what they'll get. Now that I know we're
never to see the face o' God, we have nothing to lose. So, make
sure you have your message right, Father, 'cause there will be no
other warning."
- Eddie Lenihan

"The inner revolution will not be televised or sold on the
Internet. It must take place within one's own mind and heart."

- Noah Levine

"Music and silence combine strongly because music is done with silence, and silence is full of music. "
- Marcel Marceau

"Sit tall in the saddle; hold your head up high. Keep your eyes fixed where the trail meets the sky, and live like you ain't afraid to die. And don't be scared, just enjoy your ride."
- Chris Ledoux

"How far is too far? When you love a band so much that its songs fill the empty spaces inside your head and heart, is that too far?"
- Bert Murray

"Bitch power is the juice, the sweat, the blood that keeps pop music going. Rick James helped me understand the lesson of the eighth-grade dance: Bitch power rules the world. If the girls don't like the music, they sit down and stop the show. You gotta have a crowd if you wanna have a show. And the girls are the show. We're talking absolute monarchy, with no rules of succession. Bitch power. She must be obeyed. She must be feared."
- Rob Sheffield

"It was a kind of sado-masochism. I would take the things that were painful to me and elevate them and, through the mantra of music, make them into a release."
- Michael Gira

"There is no such thing as happy music."
- Franz Schubert

"Life is a beach-I'm just playin in the sand"
- Lil Wayne

"There is an hour of the afternoon when the plain is on the verge of saying something. It never says, or perhaps it says it infinitely, or perhaps we do not understand it, or we understand it and it is untranslatable as music."
- Jorge Luis Borges

"I used to dream, and I used to vow;
I wouldn't dream of it now."
- Morrissey

"Even I, as sick as I am, I would never be you.
Even I, sick and depraved, a traveler to the grave, I would never be you."
- Morrissey

"I was about 12 years old and I was sitting watching the television and it was some kind of talent show, you know, and on marches this monkey, this ape, in a pair of red-checked trousers with a little matching jacket holding a ukelele and it started jigging around playing it, and it was looking straight into the camera, straight at me, and I remember thinking, that's it, that'll be me, you know, that'll be me."
- Nick Cave

"When we feel, a kind of lyric is sung in our heart.
When we think, a kind of music is played in our mind.
In harmony, both create a beautiful symphony of life."
- Toba Beta

"I've got soul, but I'm not a souldier."
- The Killers

"Satan rejected my soul; as low as he goes,
he never quite goes this low."
- Morrissey

"A doctor, a logician and a marine biologist had also just arrived, flown in at phenomenal expense from Maximegalon to try to reason with the lead singer who had locked himself in the bathroom with a bottle of pills and was refusing to come out till it could be proved conclusively to him that he wasn't a fish. The bass player was busy machine-gunning his bedroom and the drummer was nowhere on board.
Frantic inquiries led to the discovery that he was standing on a beach on Santraginus V over a hundred light years away where, he claimed, he had been happy for over half an hour now and had found a small stone that would be his friend."
- Douglas Adams

"I'm looking at you through the glass
Don't know how much time has past
Oh God it feels like forever
But no one tells that forever feels like home
Sitting all alone in your head"
- Stone Sour

"The Universe is making music all the time."
- Tom Waits

"The good times are killing me"
- Modest Mouse

"I refuse to believe that Hendrix had the last possessed hand,
that Joplin had the last drunken throat,
that Morrison had the last enlightened mind."
- Patti Smith

"For the record, folks; I never took a shit on stage and the closest I ever came to eating shit anywhere was at a Holiday Inn buffet in Fayetteville, North Carolina, in 1973."
- Frank Zappa

"I never liked jazz music because jazz music doesn't resolve. But I was outside the Bagdad Theater in Portland one night when I saw a man playing the saxophone. I stood there for fifteen minutes, and he never opened his eyes."
- Donald Miller

"There must be some kind of way out of here,' said the joker to the thief..."
- Bob Dylan

"When you can write music that endures, bravo. Until then, keep quiet and study the work of those who can."
- Jennifer Donnelly

"My first wife said, 'It's either that
guitar or me,' you know -- and I give
you three guesses which one went."
- Jeff Beck

"Perfume was first created to mask the stench of foul and offensive odors...
Spices and bold flavorings were created to mask the taste of putrid and rotting meat...
What then was music created for?
Was it to drown out the voices of others, or the voices within ourselves?
I think I know."
- Emilie Autumn

"We are the music-makers,
And we are the dreamers of dreams,
Wandering by lone sea-breakers,
And sitting by desolate streams.
World-losers and world-forsakers,

Upon whom the pale moon gleams;
Yet we are the movers and shakers,
Of the world forever, it seems."
- Arthur O'Shaughnessy

"A song can take you back instantly to a moment, or a place, or even a person. No matter what else has changed in you or the world, that one song stays the same, just like that moment. Which is pretty amazing, when you actually think about it."
- Sarah Dessen

"Music with dinner is an insult both to the cook and the violinist."
- G.K. Chesterton

"This above all: to thine own self be true,
And it must follow, as the night the day,
Thou canst not then be false to any man."
- William Shakespeare

"Well you found us strength and solutions but I liked the tension
And not always knowing the answers when you're gonna lose it, you're gonna lose it."
- Hayley Williams

"And, in the end
The love you take
is equal to the love you make."
- Paul McCartney

"Music is what tell us that the human race is greater than we realize."
- Napoleon

"Tone of colour in a room or a morning sky, a particular perfume that you had once loved and that brings subtle

memories with it, a line from a forgotten poem that you had come across again, a cadence from a piece of music that you had ceased to play? I tell you, Dorian, that it is on things like these that our lives depend."
- Oscar Wilde

"I believe that music is a force in itself. It is there and it needs an outlet, a medium. In a way, we are just the medium."
- Maynard James Keenan

"Those who dance are considered insane by those who cannot hear the music."
- George Carlin

"Music expresses that which cannot be put into words and that which cannot remain silent"
- Victor Hugo

"People haven't always been there for me but music always has."
- Taylor Swift

"None but ourselves can free our minds."
- Bob Marley

"If I were not a physicist, I would probably be a musician. I often think in music. I live my daydreams in music. I see my life in terms of music."
- Albert Einstein

"Music was my refuge. I could crawl into the space between the notes and curl my back to loneliness."
- Maya Angelou

"After silence, that which comes nearest to expressing the inexpressible is music."

- Aldous Huxley

"We are the music makers, and we are the dreamers of dreams."
- Arthur O'Shaughnessy

"Without deviation from the norm, progress is not possible."
- Frank Zappa

"Music is to the soul what words are to the mind."
- Modest Mouse

"Life's temptations have the purpose of putting our spiritual
integrity to the test. To yield to them, however, gives one a
precarious and tormented satisfaction. But the worst temptations
are those we give in to without getting anything in return except
for the brutal discovery of our weakness."
- Paolo Maurensig

"For the first time, he heard something that he knew to be music.
He heard people singing. Behind him, across vast distances of
space and time, from the place he had left, he thought he heard
music too. But perhaps, it was only an echo."
- Lois Lowry

"Life, he realize, was much like a song. In the beginning there is
mystery, in the end there is confirmation, but it's in the middle
where all the emotion resides to make the whole thing
worthwhile."
- Nicholas Sparks

"And those who were seen dancing were thought to be insane by
those who could not hear the music."
- Friedrich Nietzsche

"People worry about kids playing with guns, and teenagers
watching violent videos; we are scared that some sort of culture
of violence will take them over. Nobody worries about kids

listening to thousands - literally thousands - of songs about broken hearts and rejection and pain and misery and loss."
- Nick Hornby

"If I should ever die, God forbid, let this be my epitaph:
THE ONLY PROOF HE NEEDED FOR THE EXISTENCE OF GOD WAS MUSIC"
- Kurt Vonnegut

"Life is for the living.
Death is for the dead.
Let life be like music.
And death a note unsaid."
- Langston Hughes

"We should consider every day lost on which we have not danced at least once."
- Friedrich Nietzsche

"It's no good pretending that any relationship has a future if your record collections disagree violently or if your favorite films wouldn't even speak to each other if they met at a party."
- Nick Hornby

"Somebody just gave me a shower radio. Thanks a lot. Do you really want music in the shower? I guess there's no better place to dance than a slick surface next to a glass door."
- Jerry Seinfeld

"The only escape from the miseries of life are music and cats..."
- Albert Schweitzer

"Play it fuckin' loud!"
- Bob Dylan

"Music gives a soul to the universe, wings to the mind, flight to the imagination

and life to everything."
- Plato

"You have enemies? Good, that means you stood up for something."
- Eminem

"Music is ... A higher revelation than all Wisdom & Philosophy"
- Ludwig van Beethoven

"To stop the flow of music would be like the stopping of time itself, incredible and inconceivable."
- Aaron Copland

"Everybody has that point in their life where you hit a crossroads and you've had a bunch of bad days and there's different ways you can deal with it and the way I dealt with it was I just turned completely to music."
- Taylor Swift

"If you're going to kick authority in the teeth, you might as well use two feet."
- Keith Richards

"Music . . . can name the unnameable and communicate the unknowable."
- Leonard Bernstein

"And I thought about how many people have loved those songs. And how many people got through a lot of bad times because of those songs. And how many people enjoyed good times with those songs. And how much those songs really mean. I think it would be great to have written one of those songs. I bet if I wrote one of them, I would be very proud. I hope the people who wrote those songs are happy. I hope they feel it's enough. I really do because they've made me happy. And I'm only one person."
- Stephen Chbosky

"If you look in the mirror and don't like what you see, you can find out first hand what it's like to be me."
- Gerard Way

"Have you got any soul?" a woman asks the next afternoon. That depends, I feel like saying; some days yes, some days no. A few days ago I was right out; now I've got loads, too much, more than I can handle. I wish I could spread it a bit more evenly, I want to tell her, get a better balance, but I can't seem to get it sorted. I can see she wouldn't be interested in my internal stock control problems though, so I simply point to where I keep the soul I have, right by the exit, just next to the blues."
- Nick Hornby

"I had a boyfriend who told me I'd never succeed, never be nominated for a Grammy, never have a hit song, and that he hoped I'd fail. I said to him, 'Someday, when we're not together, you won't be able to order a cup of coffee at the fucking deli without hearing or seeing me."
- Lady Gaga

"Why do beautiful songs make you sad?' 'Because they aren't true.' 'Never?' 'Nothing is beautiful and true."
- Jonathan Safran Foer

"The only truth is music."
- Jack Kerouac

"I accept chaos, I'm not sure whether it accepts me."
- Bob Dylan

"Everything in the universe has a rhythm, everything dances. "
- Maya Angelou

"I haven't understood a bar of music in my life, but I have felt it."
- Igor Stravinsky

"But I was not in the band, because I suffer from the kind of tone deafness that is generally associated with actual deafness"
- John Green

"Music is the divine way to tell beautiful, poetic things to the heart.."
- Pablo Casals

"I hope they understand that I'm not angry, I'm just saying... Sometimes goodbye is a second chance."
- Shinedown

"People are talking about immigration, emigration and the rest of the fucking thing. It's all fucking crap. We're all human beings, we're all mammals, we're all rocks, plants, rivers. Fucking borders are just such a pain in the fucking arse."
- Shane MacGowan

"Somebody said to me, 'But the Beatles were anti-materialistic.' That's a huge myth. John and I literally used to sit down and say, 'Now, let's write a swimming pool."
- Paul McCartney

"Freedom's just a word today
Freedom's just a word
When someone takes your word away
It's seldom ever heard
So take a sentence full of things you're not supposed to say
Carry on, but don't write them down or you'll be gone"
- Stone Sour

"I've been trying to start a garage band for over a decade now, but father won't move his car."

- Jarod Kintz

"Ignore all hatred and criticism. Live for what you create, and die protecting it."
- Lady Gaga

"Music sounds different to the one who plays it. It is the musician's curse."
- Patrick Rothfuss

"My new album that I'm creating, which is finished pretty much, was written with this new instinctual energy that I've developed getting to know my fans. They protect me, so now it's my destiny to protect them."
- Lady Gaga

"Tax not so bad a voice to slander music any more than once."
- William Shakespeare

"Live your truth. Express your love. Share your enthusiasm. Take action towards your dreams. Walk your talk. Dance and sing to your music. Embrace your blessings. Make today worth remembering."
- Steve Maraboli

"Film as dream, film as music. No art passes our conscience in the way film does, and goes directly to our feelings, deep down into the dark rooms of our souls."
- Ingrid Bergman

"The voice so filled with nostalgia that you could almost see the memories floating through the blue smoke, memories not only of music and joy and youth, but perhaps, of dreams. They listened to the music, each hearing it in his own way, feeling relaxed and a part of the music, a part of each other, and almost a part of the world. "

- Hubert Selby Jr.

"Some might tell you there's no hope in hand
Just because they feel hopeless
But you don't have to be a thing like that
You be a ship in a bottle set sail "
- Dave Matthews Band

"Lose your dream, you lose your mind."
- The Rolling Stones

"You better start swimming, or you'll sink like a stone. Because
the Time's they are a-changing."
- Bob Dylan

"Music, my rampart and my only one."
- Edna St. Vincent Millay

Miguel de Cervantes Saavedra
"He who sings scares away his woes."
- Miguel de Cervantes Saavedra

"I'm just a musical prostitute, my dear."
- Freddie Mercury

"But you'll always be my hero
even though you've lost your mind
Now there's gravel in our voices
glass is shattered from the fight
in this tug of war, you'll always win
even when I'm right
'cause you feed me fables from your hand
with violent words and empty threats"
- Rihanna

"If you've lost your faith in love and music then the end won't be
long."

- Pete Doherty

"If I cannot fly, let me sing."
- Stephen Sondheim

"I'd love to...but only with you."
- Morrissey

"I found my God in music and the arts, with writers like
Hermann Hesse, and musicians like Muddy Waters, Howlin'
Wolf, and Little Walter. In some way, in some form, my God
was always there, but now I have learned to talk to him."
- Eric Clapton

"Songs, to me, were more important than just light
entertainment. They were my preceptor and guide into some
altered consciousness of reality. Some different republic, some
liberated republic... whatever the case, it wasn't that I was anti-
popular culture or anything and I had no ambition to stir things
up. I just thought of mainstream culture as lame as hell and a big
trick. It was like the unbroken sea of frost that lay outside the
window and you had to have awkward footgear to walk with."
- Bob Dylan

"The pianokeys are black and white
but they sound like a million colors in your mind"
- Maria Cristina Mena

"Can you squeeze me into an empty page of your diary and
psychologically save me?"
- Morrissey

"My choice is what I choose to do,
And if I'm causing no harm, it shouldn't bother you.
   Your choice is who you choose to be,
And if you're causing' no harm, then you're alright with me."
- Ben Harper

70

"In our world, I rank music somewhere between hair ribbons and rainbows in terms of usefulness."
- Suzanne Collins

It wasn't because the music got so bad that I quit going to Mass, but it certainly was the beginning of my doubts about papal infallibility."
- Mary Rose O'Reilley

"Excuse me if I have/some place in my mind/where I go time to time."
- Tom Petty

"I have an idea that the only thing which makes it possible to regard this world we live in without disgust is the beauty which now and then men create out of the chaos. The pictures they paint, the music they compose, the books they write, and the lives they lead. Of all these the richest in beauty is the beautiful life. That is the perfect work of art."
- W. Somerset Maugham

"Music touches us emotionally, where words alone can't."
- Johnny Depp

"There ain't no devil, only God when he's drunk."
- Tom Waits

"I'm already crazy. I'm a fearless person. I think it creeps up on you. I don't think it can be stopped. If my destiny is to lose my mind because of fame, then that's my destiny. But my passion still means more than anything."
- Lady Gaga

"When we die, we will turn into songs, and we will hear each other and remember each other."

- Rob Sheffield

"You can't be too careful anymore, when all that is waiting for you won't come any closer, you've got to reach a little more!"
- Paramore

"Heard melodies are sweet, but those unheard are sweeter: therefore, ye soft pipes, play on."
- John Keats

"Out of sorrow entire worlds have been built
Out of longing great wonders have been willed"
- Nick Cave

"Music is powerful; it transforms emotions and experiences into something tangible."
- Michelle Madow

"Through music we may wander where we will in time, and find friends in every century."
- Helen Thompson

"A middle finger is more New York than a corporate ambush. I bleed for my hometown, and I'd die for my fans."
- Lady Gaga

"I think people who truly can live a life in music are telling the world, 'You can have my love, you can have my smiles. Forget the bad parts, you don't need them. Just take the music, the goodness, because it's the very best, and it's the part I give most willingly"
- George Harrison

"I don't mind if you forget me.
Having learned my lesson,
I never left an impression on anyone."
- Morrissey

"The Monster Ball is by nature a protest: A youth church experience to speak out and celebrate against all forms of discrimination + prejudice."
- Lady Gaga

"The devil, the originator of sorrowful anxieties and restless troubles, flees before the sound of music almost as much as before the Word of God....Music is a gift and grace of God, not an invention of men. Thus it drives out the devil and makes people cheerful. Then one forgets all wrath, impurity, and other devices."
- Martin Luther

"The mosh pit will reveal all the answers. The mosh pit never lies. "
- Rachel Cohn

"Im not crazy, Im just a little unwell."
- Rob Thomas

"Thinking of a series of dreams
Where the time and the tempo fly
And there's no exit in any direction
'Except the one that you can't see with your eyes"
- Bob Dylan

"I am hated for loving.
I am haunted for wanting."
- Morrissey

"He wanted to cry quietly but not for himself: for the words, so beautiful and sad, like music."
- James Joyce

"I want what we all want," said Carl. "To move certain parts of the interior of myself into the exterior world, to see if they can be embraced."
- Jonathan Lethem

"Music does not replace words, it gives tone to the words"
- Elie Wiesel

"Don't be afraid, just play the music."
- Charlie Parker

"No one wants to admit we're addicted to music. That's just not possible. No one's addicted to music and television and radio. We just need more of it, more channels, a larger screen, more volume. We can't bear to be without it, but no, nobody's addicted. We could turn it off anytime we wanted. I fit a window frame into a brick wall. With a little brush, the size for fingernail polish, I glue it. The window is the size of a fingernail. The glue smells like hair spray. The smell tastes like oranges and gasoline."
- Chuck Palahniuk

"To be creative means to be in love with life. You can be creative only if you love life enough that you want to enhance its beauty, you want to bring a little more music to it, a little more poetry to it, a little more dance to it."
- Osho

"I play until my fingers are blue and stiff from the cold, and then I keep on playing. Until I'm lost in the music. Until I am the music--notes and chords, the melody and harmony. It hurts, but it's okay because when I'm the music, I'm not me. Not sad. Not afraid. Not desperate. Not guilty."
- Jennifer Donnelly

"This sick strange darkness comes creeping on so haunting everytime.

And as I stared I counted the webs from all the spiders
catching things and eating their insides,
Like indecision to call you
And hear your voice of treason
Will you come home and stop this pain tonight stop this pain
tonight"
- Blink-182

"This is the music business. 'Five years is five hundred years' -
your words."
- Jennifer Egan

"The Ultimate Rule ought to be: 'If it sounds GOOD to you, it's
bitchin'; if it sounds BAD to YOU, it's shitty. The more your
musical experience, the easier it is to define for yourself what
you like and what you don't like. American radio listeners, raised
on a diet of _____ (fill in the blank), have experienced a musical
universe so small they cannot begin to know what they like."
- Frank Zappa

"I was wasting my life, always thinking about myself."
- Morrissey

"It's music rage, which is like road rage, only more righteous.
When you get road rage, a tiny part of you knows you're being a
jerk, but when you get music rage, you're carrying out the will of
God, and God wants these people dead"
- Nick Hornby

"Am I a mindless fool? My life is a fragment, a disconnected
dream that has no continuity. I am so tired of senselessness. I am
tired of the music that my feelings sing, the dream music."
- Ross David Burke

"With no reason to hide these words I feel, and no reason to talk
about the books I read, but still, I do."

- Morrissey

"Your promises, they look like lies. Your honesty's, like a back that hides a knife. I promise you I am finally free."
- 30 Seconds to Mars

"Carolina beach music," Dupree said, coming up on the porch. "The holiest sound on earth."
- Pat Conroy

"I love science, and it pains me to think that so many are terrified of the subject or feel that choosing science means you cannot also choose compassion, or the arts, or be awed by nature. Science is not meant to cure us of mystery, but to reinvent and reinvigorate it."
- Robert M. Sapolsky

"I am the son and the heir of a shyness that is criminally vulgar."
- Morrissey

"Music, of all the arts, stands in a special region, unlit by any star but its own, and utterly without meaning ... except its own."
- Leonard Bernstein

"Because you wear a uniform, a smelly uniform...and so you think you can be rude to me."
- Morrissey

"Don't look at the past again the first and last has made everything new, And you are too so lift your head and let your story be told.
Life on earth will end for all conceived and prove to be only a breath, A mist, a womb for what's to come. How soon forever arrives"
- Flyleaf

"Music is stored in our long-term memory. When we learn something through music, we tend to remember it longer and believe it more deeply. Dr. Joyce Brothers"
- Joyce Brothers

"Then the singing enveloped me. It was furry and resonant, coming from everyone's very heart. There was no sense of performance or judgment, only that the music was breath and food."
- Anne Lamott

"If love played an instrument, I'll bet it would be the piano. 88 keys, double infinity, and the ability to chop down trees with a sharpened mustache."
- Jarod Kintz

"I'm a super hero, too, underneath my sweater."
- Rusted Root

"It is cruel, you know, that music should be so beautiful. It has the beauty of loneliness of pain: of strength and freedom. The beauty of disappointment and never-satisfied love. The cruel beauty of nature and everlasting beauty of monotony."
- Benjamin Britten

"Burn down the disco
Hang the blessed D.J.
Because the music that they constantly play
It says nothing to me about my life"
- Morrissey

"You know I love to spend my mornings, like sunlight dancing on your skin"
- Rodney Crowell

"Sounds travel through space long after their wave patterns have ceased to be detectable by the human ear: some cut right through the ionosphere and barrel on out into the cosmic heartland, while others bounce around, eventually being absorbed into the vibratory fields of earthly barriers, but in neither case does the energy succumb; it goes on forever - which is why we, each of us, should take pains to make sweet notes."
- Tom Robbins

"Do you remember what Darwin says about music? He claims that the power of producing and appreciating it existed among the human race long before the power of speech was arrived at. Perhaps that is why we are so subtly influenced by it. There are vague memories in our souls of those misty centuries when the world was in its childhood.'
That's a rather broad idea,' I remarked.
One's ideas must be as broad as Nature if they are to interpret Nature,' he answered."
- Arthur Conan Doyle

"You made me feel less alone;
you made me feel not quite so
deformed, uninformed and hunchbacked."
- Morrissey

"A successful song comes to sing itself inside the listener. It is cellular and seismic, a wave coalescing in the mind and in the flesh. There is a message outside and a message inside, and those messages are the same, like the pat and thud of two heartbeats, one within you, one surrounding. The message of the lullaby is that it's okay to dim the eyes for a time, to lose sight of yourself as you sleep and as you grow: if you drift, it says, you'll drift ashore: if you fall, you will fall into place."
- Kevin Brockmeier

"Words make you think. Music makes you feel. A song makes you feel a thought."

- Yip Harburg

"A strange art – music – the most poetic and precise of all the arts, vague as a dream and precise as algebra."
- Guy de Maupassant

"I have my books
And my poetry to protect me;
I am shielded in my armor,
Hiding in my room, safe within my womb.
I touch no one and no one touches me.
I am a rock,
I am an island."
- Simon and Garfunkel

"Well, I sort of don't trust anybody who doesn't like Led Zeppelin."
- Jack White

"Next to the Word of God, the noble art of music is the greatest treasure in the world."
- Martin Luther

"These tears I'm wailing,
I spill not without reason.
Remove them, my dearest love.
Take me to the place I've been dreaming of,
where the grotesquely lonely
meet the grotesquely lonely
and they whisper,
just very softly,
Please be mine, Dearest Love."
- Morrissey

"The music enchanted the air. It was like the south wind, like a warm night, like swelling sails beneath the stars, completely and utterly unreal... It made everything spacious and colourful, the

dark stream of life seemed pulsing in it; there were no burdens
any more, no limits; there existed only glory and melody and
love, so that one simply could not realize that, at the same time
as this music was, outside there ruled poverty and torment and
despair."
- Erich Maria Remarque

"Im not going to change my ways, just to please you or appease
you, inside a crowd five billion proud willing to punch it out,
right, wrong, weak strong, ashes to ashes all fall down."
- Dave Matthews Band

"I want to recouncil the violence in your heart.
I want to recognize your beauty's not just a mask.
I want to exorcise the demons from your past.
I want to satisfy the undisclosed desires in your heart."
- Matthew J. Bellamy

"Music is the soundtrack of our lives."
- Dick Clark

"That was the day the ancient songs of blood and war spilled
from a hole in the sky And there was a long moment as we
listened and fell silent in our grief and then one by one, we stood
tall and came together and began to sing of life and love and all
that is good and true And I will never forget that day when the
ancient songs died because there was no one in the world to sing
them."
- Brian Andreas

"He had always wanted to write music, and he could give no
other identity to the thing he sought. If you want to know what it
is, he told himself, listen to the first phrases of Tchaikovsky's
First Concerto--or the last movement of Rachmaninoff's Second.
Men have not found the words for it, nor the deed nor the
thought, but they have found the music. Let me see that in one
single act of man on earth. Let me see it made real. Let me see

80

the answer to the promise of that music. Not servants nor those served; not altars and immolations; but the final, the fulfilled, innocent of pain. Don't help me or serve me, but let me see it once, because I need it. Don't work for my happiness, my brothers--show me yours--show me that it is possible--show me your achievement--and the knowledge will give me courage for mine."
- Ayn Rand

"And if the cloud bursts, thunder in your ear, you shout and no one seems to hear. And if the band you're in starts playing different tunes, I'll see you on the dark side of the moon."
- Pink Floyd

"Anything can become music if listened to long enough"
- Jeff Noon

"Wagner's music is better than it sounds."
- Bill Nye

"As the strings of a lute are apart though they quiver the same music."
- Kahlil Gibran

"I am telling you what I know -- words have music and if you are a musician you will write to hear them."
- E.L. Doctorow

"What's my age again?"
- Blink-182

"Music gives color to the air of the moment."
- Karl Lagerfeld

"The battle with the bottle is nothing so novel."
- Elvis Costello

"The emotions - love, mirth, the heroic, wonder, tranquility, fear, anger, sorrow, disgust - are in the audience."
- John Cage

"If music be the food of love, play on."
- William Shakespeare

"The heart has a heart of its own."
- Morrissey

"And the night shall be filled with music,
And the cares, that infest the day,
Shall fold their tents like the Arabs,
and silently steal away."
- Henry Wadsworth Longfellow

"Pools of sorrow waves of joy are drifting thorough my open mind possessing and caressing me"
- John Lennon

"Heaven help the roses if the bombs begin to fall"
- Stevie Wonder

"Music, once admitted to the soul, becomes a sort of spirit, and never dies."
- Edward Bulwer Lytton

"Too bad people can't always be playing music, maybe then there wouldn't be any more wars."
- Margot Benary-Isbert

"Music, when soft voices die, vibrates in the memory."
- Percy Bysshe Shelley

"Don't leave it all unsaid,
somewhere in the wasteland of your head."
- Morrissey

"Tell me what you listen to, and I'll tell you who you are."
- Tiffanie DeBartolo

"Now this might disturb you, but I find I'm OK by myself; and I don't need you or your benevolence to make sense."
- Morrissey

"Music is a proud, temperamental mistress. Give her the time and attention she deserves, and she is yours. Slight her and there will come a day when you call and she will not answer. So I began sleeping less to give her the time she needed."
- Patrick Rothfuss

"Music is the mediator between the spiritual and the sensual life."
- Ludwig van Beethoven

"A gentleman is someone who knows how to play the banjo and doesn't."
- Mark Twain

"I am human and I need to be loved, just like everybody else does."
- Morrissey

"Music is the literature of the heart; it commences where speech ends."
- Alphonse de Lamartine

"Softly, deftly, music shall caress you. Hear it, feel it, Secretly possess you."
- Andrew Lloyd Webber

"She sat listening to the music. It was a symphony of triumph. The notes flowed up, they spoke of rising and they were the

rising itself, they were the essence and the form of upward motion, they seemed to embody every human act and thought that had ascent as its motive. It was a sunburst of sound, breaking out of hiding and spreading open. It had the freedom of release and the tension of purpose. It swept space clean, and left nothing but the joy of an unobstructed effort. Only a faint echo within the sounds spoke of that from which the music had escaped, but spoke in laughing astonishment at the discovery that there was no ugliness or pain, and there never had to be. It was the song of an immense deliverance."
- Ayn Rand

"You take the breath right out of me
You left a hole where my heart should be"
- Breaking Benjamin

"There is nothing stable in the world; uproar's your only music."
- John Keats

"When I hear Jazz, my first instinct is to lean over to the guy next to me and whisper, "Fourth floor, please."
- Jarod Kintz

"How can anybody say they know how I feel? The only one around here who is me, is ME."
- Morrissey

"And these children that you spit on as they try to change their worlds are immune to your consultations.
They're quite aware of what they're going through..."
- David Bowie

"To me, the greatest pleasure of writing is not what it's about, but the music the words make."
- Truman Capote

"We are not just Art for Michelangelo to carve, he can't rewrite the agro of my furied heart"
- Lady Gaga

"You can't kick me down, I'm already on the ground. No, you can't, but you couldn't catch me anyhow.Blue skies, but the sun isn't comming out, no. Today, it is like I'm under a heavy cloud."
- Avril Lavigne

"Rejection is one thing - but rejection from a fool is cruel."
- Morrissey

"It would be inappropiate, undignified, at 38, to conduct friendships or love affairs with the ardour or intensity of a 22 year old. Falling in love like that? Writing poetry? Crying at pop songs? Dragging people into photobooths? Taking a whole day to make a compilation tape? Asking people if they wanted to share your bed, just for company? If you quoted Bob Dylan or TS Eliot or, god forbid, Brecht at someone these days they would smile politely and step quietly backwards, and who would blame them? Ridiculous, at 38, to expect a song or book or film to change your life."
- David Nicholls

"Contrary to what you may have heard from Henry Rollins or/and Ian MacKaye and/or anyone else who joined a band after working in an ice cream shop, you can't really learn much about a person based on what kind of music they happen to like. As a personality test, it doesn't work even half the time. However, there is at least one thing you can learn: The most wretched people in the word are those who tell you they like every kind of music 'except country.' People who say that are boorish and pretentious at the same time."
- Chuck Klosterman

"I can feel the night beginning, seperating me from the living.

Understanding me, after all I've seen."
- Evanescence

"I suppose it's not a social norm, and not a manly thing to do —
to feel, discuss feelings. So that's what I'm giving the finger to.
Social norms and stuff…what good are social norms, really? I
think all they do is project a limited and harmful image of
people. It thus impedes a broader social acceptance of what
someone, or a group of people, might actually be like."
- Jess C. Scott

"Please, touch me, I pray."
- Jess C. Scott

"Prejudice is a disease. And when they come for you, or refuse
your worth, I will be ready for their stones. I belong to you."
- Lady Gaga

"Oh, I can't help quoting you, because everything that you said
rings true."
- Morrissey

"I'll bet she's beautiful, that girl he talks about, and she's got
everything that I have to live without... He's the reason for the
teardrops on my guitar, the only one who's got enough of me to
break my heart. He's the song in the car I keep singing; don't
know why I do."
- Taylor Swift

"A man should hear a little music, read a little poetry, and see a
fine picture every day of his life, in order that worldly cares may
not obliterate the sense of the beautiful which God has implanted
in the human soul."
- Johann Wolfgang von Goethe

"If we communicated with something like music, we would never be misunderstood, because there is nothing in music to understand...... But until we find this new way of speaking, until we can find a nonapproximate vocabulary, nonsense words are the best thing we've got. Ifactifice is one such word."
- Jonathan Safran Foer

"You couldn't not like someone who liked the guitar."
- Stephen King

"You can't copy anybody and end with anything. If you copy, it means you're working without any real feeling. No two people on earth are alike, and it's got to be that way in music or it isn't music."
- Billie Holiday

"Without music, life would be a blank to me."
- Jane Austen

"It's the heart that really matters in the end."
- Rob Thomas

"Those guys who want to have the Mohawk...which, to me, is the new business casual."
- Gerard Way

"I was wasting my time, praying for love.
For a love that never comes, from someone who does not exist."
- Morrissey

"sometimes we take action, sometimes we take pills."
- Fall Out Boy

"Any good music must be an innovation. "
- Les Baxter

"Jazz isn't dead. It just smells funny."
- Frank Zappa

"If I can't dance to it, it's not my revolution."
- Emma Goldman

"A painter paints pictures on canvas. But musicians paint their pictures on silence."
- Leopold Stokowski

"Because when he sings...even the birds stop to listen."
- Suzanne Collins

"The truth is you don't know what is going to happen tomorrow. Life is a crazy ride, and nothing is guaranteed."
- Eminem

"And I'll stand on the ocean until I start sinking."
- Bob Dylan

"For those of you in the cheap seats I'd like ya to clap your hands to this one; the rest of you can just rattle your jewelry!"
- John Lennon

"Music makes one feel so romantic - at least it always gets on one's nerves - which is the same thing nowadays."
- Oscar Wilde

"I'm a little bit naked, but that's okay."
- Lady Gaga

"I still don't belong to anyone - I am mine."
- Morrissey

"I felt like an animal, and animals don't know sin, do they?"
- Jess C. Scott

"They say music can alter moves and talk to you. Well can it
load a gun up for you and cock it too? WIll if it can and the next
time you assault a dude, just tell the judge it was my fault...and
I'll get sued!"
- Eminem

"Music is the strongest form of magic."
- Marilyn Manson

"Hello there, the angel from my nightmare.
the shadow in the background of the morgue.
the unsuspecting victim of darkness in the valley.
we could live like jack and sally if we want."
- Blink-182

"I just can't listen to any more Wagner, you know...I'm starting
to get the urge to conquer Poland."
- Woody Allen

"The past is only the future with the lights on."
- Blink-182
"Some people have lives; some people have music."
- John Green

"Hard to say what's right when all I wanna do is wrong."
- Prince

"Life's greatest tragedy is not that it will someday end, but that
most only live to follow directions and sometimes we end up
totally lost."
- Alex Gaskarth

"If you feel so empty
So used up, so let down
If you feel so angry
So ripped off so stepped on

You're not the only one
Refusing to back down
You're not the only one
So get up"
- Three Days Grace

"And you're the only one who knows."
- Billy Joel

"He took his pain and turned it into something beautiful. Into something that people connect to. And that's what good music does. It speaks to you. It changes you."
- Hannah Harrington

"He has Van Gogh's ear for music."
- Billy Wilder

"Music is the one incorporeal entrance into the higher world of knowledge which comprehends mankind but which mankind cannot comprehend."
- Ludwig van Beethoven

"She was clean": no piercings, tattoos, or scarifications. All the kids were now. And who could blame them, Alex thought, after watching three generations of flaccid tattoos droop like moth-eaten upholstery over poorly stuffed biceps and saggy asses?"
- Jennifer Egan

"I'd wear any of my private attire for the world to see. But I would rather have an open flesh wound than ever wear a band aid in public."
- Lady Gaga

"Who can fail to mist at Fergie's anthem, 'My humps, my humps, my lovely lady lumps.' Hmmm. 'My lunch, my lunch, I swear it's coming up."
- Celia Rivenbark

"Music is the art of thinking with sounds."
- Jules Combarieu

"And the leaves were telling secrets to the wind."
- Peter Mulvey

"[The Head of Radio Three] had been ensnared by the Music Director of the college and a Professor of Philosophy. These two were busy explaining to the harassed man that the phrase "too much Mozart" was, given any reasonable definition of those three words, an inherently self-contradictory expression, and that any sentence which contained such a phrase would be thereby rendered meaningless and could not, consequently, be advanced as part of an argument in favour of any given programme-scheduling strategy."
- Douglas Adams

"Jazz is not just 'Well, man, this is what I feel like playing.' It's a very structured thing that comes down from a tradition and requires a lot of thought and study."
- Wynton Marsalis

"Because I hate the ocean, theme parks and airplanes, talking with strangers, waiting in line. I'm through with these pills that make me sit still, are you feeling fine? Yes, I feel just fine."
- Motion City Soundtrack

"Sometimes I am two people. Johnny is the nice one. Cash causes all the trouble. They fight."
- Johnny Cash

"Beethoven can write music, thank God - but he can do nothing else on earth."
- Ludwig van Beethoven

91

"Anyone who tells a lie has not a pure heart, and cannot make a good soup. "
- Ludwig van Beethoven

"Never compromise yourself. You are all you've got."
- Janis Joplin

"I think imagination is at the heart of everything we do. Scientific discoveries couldn't have happened without imagination. Art, music, and literature couldn't exist without imagination. And so anything that strengthens imagination, and reading certainly does that, can help us for the rest of our lives."
- Lloyd Alexander

"If you wanna make friends at the ATM, do the creep."
- Lonely Island

"You can love a song, but you can form a bond with an album, a relationship that evolves as organically and beautifully as a marriage."
- Jacob Hoye

"Nathan, how can you stand playing the same piece over and over again?" And Grandpa Nate answered, "Why don't you ask me how I can stand making love to the same woman over and over again?"
- E.L. Konigsburg

"A choir is made up of many voices, including yours and mine. If one by one all go silent then all that will be left are the soloists. Don't let a loud few determine the nature of the sound. It makes for poor harmony and diminishes the song."
- Vera Nazarian

"I mentally shake hands with you for your answer, despite its inaccuracy." Mr. Rochester"
- Charlotte Brontë

"The woman of my dreams - she never came along.
The woman of my dreams - well, there never was one."
- Morrissey

"The finest fury is the most controlled."
- Christopher Hitchens

"I was totally clueless about social interaction, and completely
scared of girls. All I knew was that music was going to make
girls fall in love with me."
- Rob Sheffield

"I would teach children music, physics, and philosophy; but
most importantly music, for the patterns in music and all the arts
are the keys to learning"
- Plato

"I discovered the miracle that all things that sound are music,
including the dishes and silverware in the dishwasher, as long as
they fulfill the illusion of showing us where life is heading."
- Gabriel García Márquez

"He was depressed. He was addicted to heroin. And I think there
comes a time when all the beauty in the world just isn't enough."
- Antony John

"The most exciting rhythms seem unexpected and complex, the
most beautiful melodies simple and inevitable."
- W.H. Auden

"To remember love after long sleep; to turn again to poetry after
a year in the market place, or to youth after resignation to
drowsy and stiffening age; to remember what once you thought
life could hold, after telling over with muddied and calculating
fingers what it has offered; this is music, made after long silence.

The soul flexes its wings, and, clumsy as any fledgling, tries the air again"
- Mary Stewart

"If I could be who you wanted, all the time"
- Radiohead

"From the first note I knew it was different from anything I had ever heard.... It began simply, but with an arresting phrase, so simple, but eloquent as a human voice. It spoke, beckoning gently as it unwound, rising and tensing. It spiraled upward, the tension growing with each repeat of the phrasing, and yet somehow it grew more abandoned, wilder with each note. His eyes remained closed as his fingers flew over the strings, spilling forth surely more notes than were possible from a single violin. For one mad moment I actually thought there were more of them, an entire orchestra of violins spilling out of this one instrument. I had never heard anything like it--it was poetry and seduction and light and shadow and every other contradiction I could think of. It seemed impossible to breathe while listening to that music, and yet all I was doing was breathing, quite heavily. The music itself had become as palpable a presence in that room as another person would have been--and its presence was something out of myth."
- Deanna Raybourn

"Should I have taken him by the hand and led him over to the Zappa? No. I won't spoon-feed the customers. If you don't know your alphabet, you have no business leaving your house, let alone shopping for premium music."
- Yvonne Prinz

"I am kind of majoring in bull shitting."
- Kate Voegele

""I hate happy music, that makes me sad. Sad music makes me happy."
- Ville Valo

"We imagined ourselves as the Sons of Liberty with a mission to preserve, protect, and project the revolutionary spirit of rock and roll. We feared that the music which had given us sustenance was in danger of spiritual starvation. We feared it losing its sense of purpose, we feared it falling into fattened hands, we feared it floundering in a mire of spectacle, finance, and vapid technical complexity."
- Patti Smith

"Death makes angels of us all and gives us wings where we had shoulders smooth as raven's claws."
- Jim Morrison

"We were both young when I first saw you. I close my eyes and the flashback starts. I'm standin' there on a balcony in summer air."
- Taylor Swift

"I'm coming out of my cage and I've been doing just fine. Gotta, gotta be down because I want it all. It started out with a kiss. How did it end up like this? It was only a kiss, it was only a kiss. Now I'm falling asleep and she's calling a cab; while he's having a smoke and she's taking a drag. Now they're going to bed and my stomach is sick and it's all in my head, but she's touching his chest. Now, he takes off her dress. Now, letting me go and I just can't look - it's killing me and taking control. Jealousy, turning saints into the sea,swimming through sick lullabies. Choking on your alibis, but it's just the price I pay. Destiny is calling me. Open up my eager eyes 'cause I'm Mr. Brightside."
- The Killers

"Everything on the radio is crap...It's fast food for your ears. It doesn't make you think. It isn't even about anything - not anything real. Don't you think music should say something?"
- Hannah Harrington

"The Show Must Go On!"
- Queen

"I have always been resistant to doctrine, and any spirituality I had experienced thus far in my life had been much more abstract and not aligned with any recognized religion. For me, the most trustworthy vehicle for spirituality had always proven to be music. It cannot be manipulated, or politicized, and when it is, that becomes immediately obvious."
- Eric Clapton

"No matter who we are, no matter what our circumstances, our feelings and emotions are universal. And music has always been a great way to make people aware of that connection. It can help you open up a part of yourself and express feelings you didn't know you were feeling. It's risky to let that happen. But it's a risk you have to take-because only then will you find you're not alone."
- Josh Groban

"They may not like us, but they can't get away from knowing who we are."
- Robert Smith

"Strange how potent cheap music is."
- Noël Coward

"If I knew I was going to die at a specific moment in the future, it would be nice to be able to control what song I was listening to; this is why I always bring my iPod on airplanes."
- Chuck Klosterman

"It's like if the music is loud enough I won't be able to listen to my own thoughts. "
- Nic Sheff

"People ask me how I make music. I tell them I just step into it. It's like stepping into a river and joining the flow. Every moment in the river has its song."
- Michael Jackson

"Thank God for books and music and things I can think about."
- Daniel Keyes

"Down in Louisiana we call that Boogie Woogie!"
- Jerry Lee Lewis

"Hell is full of musical amateurs: music is the brandy of the damned. May not one lost soul be permitted to abstain?"
- George Bernard Shaw

"I will never let you fall
I'll stand up with you forever
I'll be there for you through it all
Even if saving you sends me to heaven"
- The Red Jumpsuit Apparatus

"The artist must forget the audience,
forget the critics, forget the technique, forget everything but love for the music.
Then, the music speaks through the performance,
and the performer and the listener will walk together
with the soul of the composer, and with God."
- Mstislav Rostropovich

"So I would choose to be with you,
That's if the choice were mine to make,
But you can make decisions too,
And you can have this heart to break"

- Billy Joel

"Shoot for the stars, so if you fall you land on a cloud."
- Kanye West

"We get a little further from perfection,
each year on the road,
I guess that's what they call character,
I guess that's just the way it goes,
better to be dusty than polished,
like some store window mannequin,
why don't you touch me where I'm rusty,
let me stain your hands"
- Ani DiFranco

"Life is like a beautiful melody, only the lyrics are messed up."
- Hans Christian Andersen

"Our lives were just beginning, our favorite moment was right
now, our favorite songs were unwritten."
- Rob Sheffield

"It's not that we have to quit this life one day, but it's how many
things we have to quit all at once: music, laughter, the physics of
falling leaves, automobiles, holding hands, the scent of rain, the
concept of subway trains... if only one could leave this life
slowly!"
- Roman Payne

"We grown-up people think that we appreciate music, but if we
realized the sense that an infant has brought with it of
appreciating sound and rhythm, we would never boast of
knowing music. The infant is music itself."
- Hazrat Inayat Khan

"Music can change the world because it can change people."

- Bono

"To me you are a work of art, and I would give you my heart - that's if I had one."
- Morrissey

"Most people die with their music still locked up inside them."
- Benjamin Disraeli

"Life is but a dream for the dead."
- Gerard Way

"I always felt that Jim Morrison was a terrible name for the front man of The Doors. No, for a band called The Doors, a name like Rusty Hinge would have been more appropriate."
- Jarod Kintz

"I see my life in terms of music."
- Albert Einstein

"Music is the moonlight in the gloomy night of life."
- Friedrich Richter

"I took your matches before fire could catch me, so don't look now. I'm shining like fireworks over your sad, empty town."
- Taylor Swift

"Life seems to go on without effort when I am filled with music."
- George Eliot

"This machine kills fascists."
- Woody Guthrie

"You're gonna catch a cold from the ice inside your soul"
- Christina Perri

"I know I'm an acquired taste - I'm anchovies. And not everybody wants those hairy little things."
- Tori Amos

"A good compilation tape, like breaking up, is hard to do and takes ages longer than it might seem. You've got to kick off with a killer, to grab the attention. Then you've got to take it up a notch, or cool it off a notch…oh, there are a lot of rules."
- Nick Hornby

"Floating, falling, sweet intoxication. Touch me, trust me, savor each sensation. Let the dream begin, let your darker side give in to the power of the music of the night."
- Andrew Lloyd Webber

"For me there is something primitively soothing about this music, and it went straight to my nervous system, making me feel ten feet tall."
- Eric Clapton

"I could do with a bit more excess. From now on I'm going to be immoderate--and volatile--I shall enjoy loud music and lurid poetry. I shall be rampant."
- Joanne Harris

"No matter how corrupt, greedy, and heartless our government, our corporations, our media, and our religious & charitable institutions may become, the music will still be wonderful."
- Kurt Vonnegut

"It begins in the heart...and it hurts when it's true.
It only hurts because it's true."
- Morrissey

"You can live with me in this house I've built out of writers blocks."
- Pete Wentz

"I see my life in terms of music."
- Albert Einstein

"We're in the city of wonder..."
- Rihanna

"To live is to be musical, starting with the blood dancing in your veins. Everything living has a rhythm. Do you feel your music?"
- Michael Jackson

"A great song should lift your heart, warm the soul and make you feel good."
- Colbie Caillat

"My friends joke that I'm dead until I get onstage. I'm dead right now as you're speaking to me."
- Lady Gaga

"An unalterable and unquestioned law of the musical world required that the German text of French operas sung by Swedish artists should be translated into Italian for the clearer understanding of English-speaking audiences."
- Edith Wharton

"The dilemma of the eighth-grade dance is that boys and girls use music in different ways. Girls enjoy music they can dance to, music with strong vocals and catchy melodies. Boys, on the other hand, enjoy music they can improve by making up filthy new lyrics."
- Rob Sheffield

"Tried living in the real world instead of a shell, but I was bored before I even began."
- Morrissey

"Why not just live in the moment, especially if it has a good beat?"
- Goldie Hawn

"There are only a few notes. Just variations on a theme."
- John Lennon

"Time, is going by, so much faster than I. And I'm starting to regret not spending all of it with you. Now I'm wondering why, I've kept this bottled up inside. So I'm starting to regret not telling all of it to you. So if I haven't yet, I gotta let you know, you're never gonna be alone from this moment on. If you ever feel like letting go, I won't let you fall. You're never gonna be alone, I'll hold you till the hurt is gone."
- Nickelback

"So many will try to destroy me. So many, over and over, coming in periods of greatness. But in this period, I cannot be broken: GAGAKLEIN."
- Lady Gaga

"I don't like my language watered down, I don't like my edges rounded off."
- Ani DiFranco

"Mellow is the man who knows what he's been missing"
- Led Zeppelin

"The more you ignore me, the closer I get; you're wasting your time."
- Morrissey

"If you can't hold on, hold on"

- The Killers

"There are no words and there is no singing, but the music has a voice. It is an old voice and a deep voice, like the stump of a sweet cigar or a shoe with a hole. It is a voice that has lived and lives, with sorrow and shame, ecstasy and bliss, joy and pain, redemption and damnation. It is a voice with love and without love. I like the voice, and though I can't talk to it, I like the way it talks to me. It says it is all the same, Young Man. Take it and let it be."
- James Frey

"The more you love,the more love you have to give.It's the only feeling we have which is infinite..."
- Christina Westover

"Droplets of yes and no, in an ocean of maybe."
- Faith No More

"Too bad people can't always be playing music, maybe then there wouldn't be any more wars."
- Margot Benary-Isbert

"She leans into this guy and rocks her head like I'm making this music for her, when if I could, I would take it all away and give her as much silence as she's given me pain. "
- Rachel Cohn

"You dont know what you got till its gone"
- Joni Mitchell

"Last night I dreamt that somebody loved me.
No hope, no harm; just another false alarm"
- Morrissey

"Music is the only language in which you cannot say a mean or sarcastic thing."

- John Erskine

"My music isn't just music- its medicine."
- Kanye West

"It was the moment I realized what music can do to people, how it can make you hurt and feel so good all at once."
- Nina LaCour

"Sing your life; any fool can think of words that rhyme."
- Morrissey

"Music. A meaningless acceleration in the rhythm of celestial experience."
- C.S. Lewis

"She knew this music--knew it down to the very core of her being--but she had never heard it before. Unfamiliar, it had still always been there inside her, waiting to be woken. It grew from the core of mystery that gives a secret its special delight, religion its awe. It demanded to be accepted by simple faith, not dissected or questioned, and at the same time, it begged to be doubted and probed."
- Charles de Lint

"Everybody sing like it's the last song you will ever sing.
Tell me, tell me, do you feel the pressure now?
Everybody live like it's the last day you will ever see.
Tell me, tell me, do you feel the pressure now?"
- Paramore

"The shortest distance between two people is a smile."
- Victor Borge

"What you see is kinda what you get with me. I'm a very real person, or I hope to be, anyway. I don't have nothing to hide"
- Kenny Chesney

"There's so much destruction all over the world - and all you can do is complain about ME!"
- Morrissey

"Each song is a child I nourish and give my love to. But even if you have never written a song, your life is a song. How can it not be?"
- Michael Jackson

"Life is one grand sweet song so start the music"
- Ronald Reagan

"Only God can judge me so I'm gone, either love me or leave me alone."
- Jay-Z

"Close your eyes, and think of someone you physically admire, and let me kiss you."
- Morrissey
"All I want is someone I can't resist ...I will know all I need to know by the way that I got kissed"
- Aerosmith

"I know by now you think I should have straightened myself out, Thank you, drop dead!"
- Morrissey

"Amy [Winehouse] changed pop music forever, I remember knowing there was hope, and feeling not alone because of her. She lived jazz, she lived the blues."
- Lady Gaga

"Can't you see that it's just raining?
There ain't no need to go outside."
- Jack Johnson

"I declare that The Beatles are mutants. Prototypes of evolutionary agents sent by God, endowed with a mysterious power to create a new human species, a young race of laughing freemen."
- Timothy Leary

"My love, wherever you are - whatever you are - don't lose faith. I know it's gonna happen someday to you."
- Morrissey

"I remembered Owen telling me how music had saved him in Phoenix, that it drowned everything out, and it was the same for me now. As long as I had something to listen to, I could blur the things I didn't want to think about, if not block them out completely."
- Sarah Dessen

"Again, I lay awake, and I cried because of waste."
- Morrissey

"I get sentimental over the music of the '90s. Deplorable, really. But I love it all. As far as I'm concerned the '90s was the best era for music ever, even the stuff that I loathed at the time, even the stuff that gave me stomach cramps."
- Rob Sheffield

"In every heart there is a room,
A sanctuary safe and strong,
To heal the wounds from lovers past,
Until a new one comes along"
- Billy Joel

"He who hears music, feels his solitude peopled at once."
- Robert Browning

"I see the world, it makes me puke, But then I look at you and know, that somewhere there's a someone who can soothe me."

- Morrissey

"All the lonely people, where do they all come from?"
- The Beatles

"The hungry and the haunted explode in a rock'n'roll band."
- Bruce Springsteen

"There is no feeling, except the extremes of fear and grief, that does not find relief in music."
- George Eliot

"Music is a language that doesn't speak in particular words. It speaks in emotions, and if it's in the bones, it's in the bones."
- Keith Richards

"When you stick a song on a tape, you set it free."
- Rob Sheffield

"The hell with the rules. If it sounds right, then it is."
- Eddie Van Halen

"And make no mistake, my friend, your pointless life will end; but before you go, can you look at the truth?"
- Morrissey

"The music we listen to may not define who we are. But it's a damn good start."
- Jodi Picoult

"The alarm in the morning? Well, I have an old tape of Carlo Maria Giulini conducting the Vienna Philharmonic Orchestra in a perfectly transcendent version in Shubert's seventh symphony. And I've rigged it up so that at exactly 7:30 every morning it falls from the ceiling onto my face."
- Stephen Fry

"Every life has a soundtrack.
There is a tune that makes me think of the summer I spent rubbing baby oil on my stomach in pursuit of the perfect tan. There's another that reminds me of tagging along with my father on Sunday morning to pick up the New York Times. There's the song that reminds me of using fake ID to get into a nightclub; and the one that brings back my cousin Isobel's sweet sixteen, where I played Seven Minutes in Heaven with a boy whose breath smelled like tomato soup.
If you ask me, music is the language of memory."
- Jodi Picoult

"The world's continual breathing is what we hear and call silence."
- Clarice Lispector

"Know I don't hate you
Don't wanna fight you
Know I'll always love you
But right now I just don't like you
Cause you took this too far"
- Relient K

"Some of us go full circle. Some of us blindly go nowhere. The circle doesn't have to be very large to make a point, kick your ass and/or be entertaining. Remember that and stay light. Even the deaf know good music when they hear it."
- Jason Mraz

"I try to live without you,
every time I do I feel dead."
- Three Days Grace

"A composer is a guy who goes around forcing his will on unsuspecting air molecules, often with the assistance of unsuspecting musicians."

- Frank Zappa

"Hair is gray and the firers are burning. So many dreams on the shelf. You say I wanted you to be proud of me. I always wanted that myself."
- Tori Amos

"You don't like me, but you love me; either way, you're wrong."
- Morrissey

"Hold on to the world we all remember fighting for. There's still strength left in us yet.
Hold on to the world we all remember dying for. There's still hope left in it yet.....
Arise and be all that you dreamed
All that you dreamed..... "
- Flyleaf

"Will you take me as I am? Strung out on another man...California, I'm comin' home."
- Joni Mitchell

"Throw your soul through every open door..."
- Adele

"I've found that no matter what life throws at me, music softens the blow."
- Bryce W. Anderson

"Don't waste your time or time will waste you."
- Muse

"Virtually every writer I know would rather be a musician."
- Kurt Vonnegut

"Then I felt something inside me break and music began to pour out into the quiet. My fingers danced; intricate and quick they

spun something gossamer and tremulous into the circle of light our fire had made. The music moved like a spiderweb stirred by a gentle breath, it changed like a leaf twisting as it falls to the ground, and it felt like three years Waterside in Tarbean, with a hollowness inside you and hands that ached from the bitter cold."
- Patrick Rothfuss

"Music- what a powerful instrument, what a mighty weapon!"
- Maria von Trapp

"There are only two things: love, all sorts of love, with pretty girls, and the music of New Orleans or Duke Ellington. Everything else ought to go, because everything else is ugly. "
- Boris Vian

"I'm wishing he could see that music lives. Forever. That it's stronger than death. Stronger than time. And that its strength holds you together when nothing else can."
- Jennifer Donnelly

"The vibrations on the air are the breath of God speaking to man's soul. Music is the language of God. We musicians are as close to God as man can be. We hear his voice, we read his lips, we give birth to the children of God, who sing his praise. That's what musicians are."
- Stephen J. Rivele

"It might sound chauvinistic, but there is a sad reality in rock music: Bands who depend on support from females inevitably crash and burn."
- Chuck Klosterman

"Poetry, plays, novels, music, they are the cry of the human spirit trying to understand itself and make sense of our world."
- Laura Malone Elliott

"When words fail music speaks."
- Irena Huang

"It's so shameful of me: I like you."
- Morrissey

"Music heard so deeply that it is not heard at all, but you are the music while the music lasts."
- T.S. Eliot

"It was sad music. But it waved its sadness like a battle flag. It said the universe had done all it could, but you were still alive."
- Terry Pratchett

"It's easy to hate and point out everything that is wrong with the world; it is the hardest and most important work in one's life to free oneself from the bonds of fear and attachment."
- Noah Levine

"But I know just what it feels like to have a voice in the back of my head, like a face that I hold inside, face that awakes when I close my eyes, face that watches everytime I lie, face that laughs everytime I fall. (It watches EVERYTHING) ... But the face inside is hearing me, right beneath my skin."
- Linkin Park

"If you want to make beautiful music, you must play the black and the white notes together."
- Richard Nixon

"I play until my fingers are blue and stiff from the cold, and then I keep on playing. Until I'm lost in the music. Until I am the music--notes and chords, the melody and harmony. It hurts, but it's okay because when I'm the music, I'm not me. Not sad. Not afraid. Not desperate. Not guilty."
- Jennifer Donnelly

"I was flipping channels, watching this cheerleading program on MTV. They took a field hockey girl and "transformed" her into a cheerleader by the end of the show. I was just wondering: what if she liked field hockey better?"
- Jess C. Scott

"I couldn't resist him, his eyes were like yours, his hair was exactly the shade of brown.
He's just not as tall, but I couldn't tell, it was dark and I was lying down."
- Amy Winehouse

"A middle-aged woman who looked like someone's cleaning lady, a shrieking adolescent lunatic and a talkshow host with an orange face... It didn't add up. Suicide wasn't invented for people like this. It was invented for people like Virginia Woolf and Nick Drake. And Me. Suicide was supposed to be cool."
- Nick Hornby

"When I am ..... completely myself, entirely alone... or during the night when I cannot sleep, it is on such occasions that my ideas flow best and most abundantly. Whence and how these ideas come I know not nor can I force them."
- Wolfgang Amadeus Mozart

"The history of music is mortal, but the idiocy of the guitar is eternal."
- Milan Kundera

"Life is a pigsty."
- Morrissey

"I'm a fountain of blood. In the shape of a girl."
- Björk

"I'm tired again, I've tried again, and now my heart is full.

And I just can't explain...so I won't even try to."
- Morrissey

"Ah, that shows you the power of music, that magician of magician, who lifts his wand and says his mysterious word and all things real pass away and the phantoms of your mind walk before you clothed in flesh."
- Mark Twain

"You have to turn it up so that your chest shakes and the drums get in between your ribs like a heartbeat and the bass goes up your spine and fizzles your brain and all you can do is dance or spin in a circle or just scream along because you know that however this music makes you feel, it's exactly right."
- Robin Benway

"Music blows lyrics up very quickly, and suddenly they become more than art. They become pompous and they become self-conscious ... I firmly believe that lyrics have to breathe and give the audience's ear a chance to understand what's going on. Particularly in the theater, where you not only have the music, but you've got costume, story, acting, orchestra. There's a lot to take in."
- Stephen Sondheim

"We are not here to do what has already been done."
- 30 Seconds to Mars

"My ambition was to live like music."
- Mary Gaitskill

"Hell is full of musical amateurs."
- George Bernard Shaw

"The more you love music, the more music you love."
- Tom Moon

"Southern girls are God's gift to the entire male population. There is absolutely no woman finer than one raised below the mason-dixon line and once you go southern may the good Lord help you - you never go back"
- Kenny Chesney

"Music produces a kind of pleasure which human nature cannot do without."
- Confucius

"I love the way music inside a car makes you feel invisible; if you plan the stereo at max volume, it's almost like the other people can't see into your vehicle. It tints your windows, somehow."
- Chuck Klosterman

"Last night I was seriously considering whether I was a bisexual or not but I don't think so though I'm not sure if I'd like to be and argh I don't think there's anything wrong with that, if you like a person, you like the person, not their genitals."
- Jess C. Scott

"I've found time can heal most anything and you just might find who you're supposed to be."
- Taylor Swift

"Music in the soul can be heard by the universe."
- Lao Tzu

"And then one day you find
Ten years have got behind you
No one told you when to run
You missed the starting gun"
- Pink Floyd

"My head'll explode if I continue with this escapism."
- Jess C. Scott

"Disappointment came to me,
and booted me, and bruised and hurt me, but that's how people
grow up."
- Morrissey

"If you must write prose or poems, the words you use should be
your own. Don't plagiarize or take 'on loan'. There's always
someone, somewhere, with a big nose, who knows, who'll trip
you up and laugh when you fall."
- Steven Morrissey

"You've got this life and while you've got it, you'd better kiss
like you only have one moment, try to hold someone's hand like
you will never get another chance to, look into people's eyes like
they're the last you'll ever see, watch someone sleeping like
there's no time left, jump if you feel like jumping, run if you feel
like running, play music in your head when there is none, and
eat cake like it's the only one left in the world!"
- C. JoyBell C.

"I have always been resistant to doctrine, and any spirituality I
had experienced thus far in my life had been much more abstract
and not aligned with any recognized religion. For me, the most
trustworthy vehicle for spirituality had always proven to be
music. It cannot be manipulated, or politicized, and when it is,
that becomes immediately obvious."
- Eric Clapton

"Don't be a drag.
Just be a queen."
- Lady Gaga

"The true mission of the violin is to imitate the accents of the human voice, a noble mission that has earned for the violin the glory of being called the king of instruments"
- Charles-Auguste de Beriot

"Music isn't just a pleasure, a transient satisfaction. It's a need, a deep hunger; and when the music is right, it's joy. Love. A foretaste of heaven. A comfort in grief.
Is it too much to think that perhaps God speaks to us sometimes through music?
How, then, could I be so ungrateful as to refuse the message?"
- Orson Scott Card

"We are the ones who take this thing called music and line it up with this thing called time. We are the ticking, we are the pulsing, we are underneath every part of this moment. And by making the moment our own, we are rendering it timeless. There is no audience. There are no instruments. There are only bodies and thoughts and murmurs and looks. It's the concert rush to end all concert rushes, because this is what matters. When the heart races, this is what it's racing towards."
- Rachel Cohn

"Strange how potent cheap music is."
- Noël Coward

"The iPod completely changed the way people approach music."
- Karl Lagerfeld

"Because ENOUGH is TOO MUCH!
And look around ...can you blame us?!"
- Morrissey

""I hate happy music, that makes me sad. Sad music makes me happy."
- Ville Valo

"Death makes angels of us all and gives us wings where we had shoulders smooth as raven's claws."
- Jim Morrison

"We were both young when I first saw you. I close my eyes and the flashback starts. I'm standin' there on a balcony in summer air."
- Taylor Swift

"When she started to play, Steinway came down personally and rubbed his name off the piano. "
- Bob Hope

"I sense the world might be more dreamlike, metaphorical, and poetic than we currently believe--but just as irrational as sympathetic magic when looked at in a typically scientific way. I wouldn't be surprised if poetry--poetry in the broadest sense, in the sense of a world filled with metaphor, rhyme, and recurring patterns, shapes, and designs--is how the world works. The world isn't logical, it's a song."
- David Byrne

"My body is an ugly masterpiece that lives off the beauty of sound."
- Chad Sugg

"They may not like us, but they can't get away from knowing who we are."
- Robert Smith

"Everything on the radio is crap...It's fast food for your ears. It doesn't make you think. It isn't even about anything - not anything real. Don't you think music should say something?"
- Hannah Harrington

"I'm coming out of my cage and I've been doing just fine. Gotta, gotta be down because I want it all. It started out with a kiss. How did it end up like this? It was only a kiss, it was only a kiss. Now I'm falling asleep and she's calling a cab; while he's having a smoke and she's taking a drag. Now they're going to bed and my stomach is sick and it's all in my head, but she's touching his chest. Now, he takes off her dress. Now, letting me go and I just can't look - it's killing me and taking control. Jealousy, turning saints into the sea, swimming through sick lullabies. Choking on your alibis, but it's just the price I pay. Destiny is calling me. Open up my eager eyes 'cause I'm Mr. Brightside."
- The Killers

"This is a book for every fiddler who has realized halfway through playing an ancient Scottish air that the Ramones "I Wanna Be Sedated" is what folk music is really all about, and gone straight into it."
- Neil Gaiman

"Stupid cupid keeps on calling me, but I see nothing in his eyes. I miss my babe"
- George Michael

"During the struggle they will pull us down. But please, please let's use this chance to turn things around. And tonight we can truly say together we're invincible"
- Matthew Bellamy

"If you turn on TV all you see's a bunch of "what the f-cks"
Dude is dating so and so blabbering bout such and such
And that aint Jersey Shore, homie that's the news
And these the same people that supposed to be telling us the truth"
- Lupe Fiasco

"All of my most significant moments somehow involved music. It's like my life was a John Hughes film and somebody had to put together the perfect soundtrack."
- Caprice Crane

"You must always believe that life is as extraordinary as music says it is."
- Rebecca West

"Your life is a fine tuned and exceptional instrument, but like a Startovarius Violin, or a fine Martin Guitar, it can still be played badly and usually is by others. So, be careful of who you let touch the strings and what you allow to strike a chord." --Jeff (Skip) Whitaker--"
- Jeff Skip Whitaker

"We hate it when our friends become successful."
- Morrissey

"Maybe redemption has stories to tell
Maybe forgiveness is right where you fell"
- Switchfoot

"I turn the music up, I got my records on, I shut the world outside me till the lights come on, maybe the streets alight, maybe the trees are gone, I feel my heart start beating to my favorite song."
- Coldplay

"Cause I don't know how it gets better than this. You take my hand and drag me head first. Fearless!"
- Taylor Swift

"It's time, my children
When the waves rise high
When the waters run deep

When the clock strikes midnight
You'll feel the mark of Zero Hour
And you'll never be the same again"
- Lisa Mangum

"Which is more musical, a truck passing by a factory or a truck passing by a music school?
Are the people inside the school musical and the ones outside unmusical?
What if the ones inside can't hear very well, would that change my question?"
- John Cage

"Where were you? When everything was falling apart. All my days staying by the telephone. You never rang and all I needed was a call."
- The Fray

"When you move like a jellyfish rhyth don't mean nothing. You go with the flow, you don't stop. Move like a jellyfish, rhythm means nothing.You go with the flow you don't stop."
- Jack Johnson

"Saying you liked all music meant that you didn't love any."
- Lindsey Kelk

"I just want you to feel beautiful. For once in your life. Just close your eyes and I'll kiss you like there's no tomorrow."
- Jamison Parker

"Everybody told me this 'girl on the piano' thing was never going to work."
- Tori Amos

"We take gingko to sharpen our memories. We could be memorizing song lyrics instead."
- Joan Oliver Goldsmith

"When you play, never mind who listens to you."
- Robert Schumann

"Music that gentlier on the spirit lies,
Than tired eyelids upon tired eyes."
- Alfred Tennyson

"The kind of person who listens to our music doesn't want to live
a bit and die a little and find a friend. The kind of person who
listens to our music wants to live forever and die a lot and fall in
love."
- Ray Robertson

"Poetry, like jazz, is one of those dazzling diamonds of creative
industry that help human beings make sense out of the comedies
and tragedies that contextualize our lives."
- Aberjhani

"Creativity is the catalyst to the future."
- Ann Marie Frohoff

"Music is spiritual. The music business is not."
- Van Morrison

"To do what you love and are passionate about is a dream come
true, My life is consumed by music and entertainment— and it's
the best life I could ever hope for."
- Blake Lewis

"Take a music bath once or twice a week for a few seasons. You
will find it is to the soul what a water bath is to the body."
- Oliver Wendell Holmes

"Dying is the fastest route to fame for an aspiring rock star. The
dead man's melodies become profound, acquiring deep mystery
and rising into a realm beyond the reach of human criticism. In

the stopping of a heartbeat, the rocker is transformed from decadent, depraved hedonist into misunderstood genius. Aye, death and musical stardom go together like Scotland and rain."
- Mark Rice

"Some need diamonds some need love
Some need cards some need luck
Some need dollar bills lining their clothes
all I need is, all I need is two white horses in a line"
- Beck Hansen

"What we believe as human nature in actuality is human habit."
- Jewel

"Life dies but forever will there be music. Always."
- Nicholas A. McGirr

"If you have to ask what jazz is you will never know." Louis Armstrong"
- Louis Armstrong

"This song is for the guy who keeps yelling from the balcony, and it's called 'we hate you, please die."
- Bryan Lee O'Malley

"I am what I am Are you what you are or What?"
- Alanis Morissette

"There are all kinds of mix tapes. There is always a reason to make one."
- Rob Sheffield

"Music... will help dissolve your perplexities and purify your character and sensibilities, and in time of care and sorrow, will keep a fountain of joy alive in you."
- Dietrich Bonhoeffer

"Do you know people who insist they like 'all kinds of music'? That actually means they like no kinds of music."
- Chuck Klosterman

"The times you lived through, the people you shared those times with nothing brings it all to life like an old mix tape. It does a better job of storing up memories than actual brain tissue can do. Every mix tape tells a story. Put them together, and they can add up to the story of a life."
- Rob Sheffield

"Musical innovation is full of danger to the State, for when modes of music change, the laws of the State always change with them."
- Plato

"I can chase you, and I can catch you, but there is nothing I can do to make you mine."
- Morrissey

"There is no pain, you are receding.
A distant ship's smoke on the horizon.
You are only coming through in waves.
Your lips move but I can't hear what you're sayin'."
- Pink Floyd

"I Wanna Hold Your Hand.' First single. Fucking brilliant. Perhaps the most fucking brilliant song ever written. Because they nailed it. That's what everyone wants. Not 24-7 hot wet sex. Not a marriage that lasts a hundred years. Not a Porsche or a blow job or a million-dollar crib. No. They wanna hold your hand. They have a feeling that they can't hide."
- Rachel Cohn

"When a man is in despair, it means that he still believes in something."
- Dmitri Shostakovich

"If you develop an ear for sounds that are musical it is like developing an ego. You begin to refuse sounds that are not musical and that way cut yourself off from a good deal of experience."
- John Cage

"Never underestimate a girl's love for her favorite band. Never think even for a minute, that she won't defend them to her death. Because it's not just the music that makes that band her favorite. It's the guys, the gals. It's the fans. People whom of which she has interacted with thanks to the band. That band might of saved her life, or just made her smile everyday. That band has never broke her heart and has yet to leave her. No wonder she finds such joy in her music."
- Alex Gaskarth

"All the good music has already been written by people with wigs and stuff."
- Frank Zappa

"Singing songs that make you slit your wrists"
- Gerard Way

"All right so you think your ready, okay then you say this with me go! We were born for this!"
- Paramore

"You're not right in the head, and nor am I, and this is why....this is why I like you."
- Morrissey

"When I hear music, I fear no danger. I am invulnerable. I see no foe. I am related to the earliest times, and to the latest."
- Henry David Thoreau

"Maybe you could be mine / or maybe we'll be entwined / aimless in this sexless foreplay."
- Jess C. Scott

"Information is not knowledge.
Knowledge is not wisdom.
Wisdom is not truth.
Truth is not beauty.
Beauty is not love.
Love is not music.
Music is THE BEST."
- Frank Zappa

"How is it that music can, without words, evoke our laughter, our fears, our highest aspirations?"
- Jane Swan

"I shall sing a sweeter song tomorrow"
- Theocritus

"Rock 'n' roll is not red carpets and MySpace friends, rock'n'roll is dangerous and should piss people off"
- Gerard Way

"He has Van Gogh's ear for music."
- Billy Wilder

"I used to think anyone doing anything weird was weird. Now I know that it is the people that call others weird that are weird."
- Paul McCartney

"You better lose yourself
In the music
The moment
You own it
You better never let it go

You only get one shot
Do not miss your chance to blow
This opportunity comes
Once in a lifetime"
- Eminem

"Songs are as sad as the listener."
- Jonathan Safran Foer

"Ah, music! A magic far beyond all we do here!"
- J.K. Rowling

"I don't stand for black man's side, I don't stand for white man's side, I stand for God's side."
- Bob Marley

"You're like a song that I heard when I was a little kid but forgot I knew until I heard it again."
- Maggie Stiefvater

"Definition of rock journalism: People who can't write, doing interviews with people who can't think, in order to prepare articles for people who can't read."
- Frank Zappa

"When you make music or write or create, it's really your job to have mind-blowing, irresponsible, condomless sex with whatever idea it is you're writing about at the time. "
- Lady Gaga

"Without music to decorate it, time is just a bunch of boring production deadlines or dates by which bills must be paid."
- Frank Zappa

"When you move like a jellyfish rhyth don't mean nothing. You go with the flow, you don't stop. Move like a jellyfish, rhythm means nothing.You go with the flow you don't stop."
- Jack Johnson

"Music is the universal language of mankind."
- Henry Wadsworth Longfellow

"I used to date the lead singer of The Cranberries, but she cheated on me. Turns out she had some turkey on the side."
- Jarod Kintz

"If being an egomaniac means I believe in what I do and in my art or music, then in that respect you can call me that... I believe in what I do, and I'll say it."
- John Lennon

"A man is a success if he gets up in the morning and gets to bed at night, and in between he does what he wants to do."
- Bob Dylan

"Music is my higher power"
- Oliver James

"Music is the wine that fills the cup of silence."
- Robert Fripp

"Girls you've gotta know when it's time to turn the page."
- Tori Amos

"The only one who's got enough of me to break my heart."
- Taylor Swift

"I've always thought people would find a lot more pleasure in their routines if they burst into song at significant moments."
- John Barrowman

"Maybe redemption has stories to tell
Maybe forgiveness is right where you fell"
- Switchfoot

"Beause I don't know how it gets better than this. You take my
hand and drag me head first. Fearless!"
- Taylor Swift

"I just want you to feel beautiful. For once in your life. Just close
your eyes and I'll kiss you like there's no tomorrow."
- Jamison Parker

"We take gingko to sharpen our memories. We could be
memorizing song lyrics instead."
- Joan Oliver Goldsmith

"I heard that knowing a musical instrument is a great way for a
guy to improve his love life, so I picked up a flute the other day
and things are looking good. I blew a few kisses at it, and it
made some girlish noises. If it's cheap enough, I'm renting it out
tonight."
- Benson Bruno

"When you play, never mind who listens to you."
- Robert Schumann

"Poetry, like jazz, is one of those dazzling diamonds of creative
industry that help human beings make sense out of the comedies
and tragedies that contextualize our lives."
- Aberjhani

"If you have to ask what jazz is you will never know." Louis
Armstrong"
- Louis Armstrong

"Music makes me forget myself, my true condition, it carries me off into another state of being, one that isn't my own: under the influence of music I have the illusion of feeling things I don't really feel, of understanding things I don't understand, being able to do things I'm not able to do (...) Can it really be allowable for anyone who feels like it to hypnotize another person, or many other persons, and then do what he likes with them? Particularly if the hypnotist is the first unscrupulous individual who happens to come along?"
- Leo Tolstoy

"He could tell by the way animals walked that they were keeping time to some kind of music. Maybe it was the song in their own hearts that they walked to."
- Laura Adams Armer

"Life dies but forever will there be music. Always."
- Nicholas A. McGirr

"I've changed my plea to guilty, because freedom is wasted on me.
See how your rules spoil the game!"
- Morrissey

"Ambition is a dream with a V8 engine. Ain't nowhere else in the world where you can go from driving a truck to cadillac overnight"
- Elvis Presley

"Music is my God, and it is the only love that has never left me."
- Ville Valo

"All the world is made of music. We are all strings on a lyre. We resonate. We sing together."
- Joe Hill

"For you can't hear Irish tunes without knowing you're Irish, and wanting to pound that fact into the floor."
- Jennifer Armstrong

"The sheer force of the music calls for a wild audience reaction."
- Emanuel Ax

"If you learn music, you'll learn most all there is to know."
- Edger Cayce

"Diazapam (that's valium), temazepam, lithium, ECT, HRT - how long must I stay on this stuff? Don't give me anymore!"
- Morrissey

"Music expresses feeling, that is to say, gives shape and habitation to feeling, not in space but in time. To the extent that music has a history that is more than a history of its formal evolution, our feelings must have a history too. Perhaps certain qualities of feeling that found expression in music can be recorded by being notated on paper, have become so remote that we can no longer inhabit them as feelings, can get a grasp of them only after long training in the history and philosophy of music, the philosophical history of music, the history of music as a history of the feeling soul."
- J.M. Coetzee

"I showed up in L.A. with $500 and a backpack and I stayed at a shelter, so nobody handed me anything. I worked for every single thing that I have."
- Jared Leto

"Now I think I understand how this world can overcome a man."
- James Sullivan

"Musicians have always had a better understanding of love than the rest of us. Over the years they have told us that love: is like a rock, is here to stay, is all you need, will find a way, will keep us together, will tear us apart, sucks."
- Cuthbert Soup

"I'm a bluesman moving through a blues-soaked America, a blues-soaked world, a planet where catastrophe and celebration-joy and pain sit side by side. The blues started off in some field, some plantation, in some mind, in some imagination, in some heart. The blues blew over to the next plantation, and then the next state. The blues went south to north, got electrified and even sanctified. The blues got mixed up with jazz and gospel and rock and roll."
- Cornel West

"We have a lot of questions, and we
want to understand.
Music helps with that .
Music helps with everything."
- Lisa Schroeder

"But there was a discipline, it was just that we didn't understand. We thought he was formless, but I think now he was tormented by order, what was outside it. He tore apart the plot - see his music was immediately on top of his own life. Echoing. As if, when he was playing he was lost and hunting for the right accidental notes. Listening to him was like talking to Coleman. You were both changing direction with every sentence, sometimes in the middle, using each other as a springboard through the dark. You were moving so fast it was unimportant to finish and clear everything. He would be describing something in 27 ways. There was pain and gentleness everything jammed into each number."
- Michael Ondaatje

"The piano ain't got no wrong notes."

- Thelonious Monk

"We live in a generation of not being in love, and not being together. But we sure make it feel like we're together, because we're scared of seeing each other with somebody else."
- Drake

"I don't feel any shame I won't apologize if there ain't nowhere you can go running away from pain when you've been victimized tales from another broken home."
- Billie Joe Armstrong

"Music fathoms the sky."
- Charles Baudelaire

"(regarding the prelude from suite two)... The key is minor, the three notes a tragic triad. The tones move closer and closer to a harrowing vision, weaving spiter-like, relentlessly gathering sound into thighter concentric circle that come to an abrupt stop. Nothing fills the empty space. A tiny prayer is uttered."
- Eric Siblin

"Your youth is the most important thing you will ever have. It's when you will connect to music like a primal urge, and the memories attached to the songs will never leave you. Please hold on to everything. Keep every note, mix tape, concert ticket stub, and memory you have of music from your youth. It'll be the one thing that might keep you young, even if you aren't anymore."
- Butch Walker

"If you were lucky enough to be different, don't ever change"
- Taylor Swift

"The tune was wailing and mournful, almost flagrantly so, and the total effect was of a heartbroken piccolo being parted forever from its bagpipe lover."
- Peter S. Beagle

"Next to the Word of God, music deserves the highest praise. The gift of language combined with the gift of song was given to man that he should proclaim the Word of God through Music."
- Martin Luther

"Music takes me to places of illimitable sensual and insensate joy, accessing points of ecstasy that no angelic lover could ever locate, or plunging me into gibbering weeping hells of pain that no torturer could ever devise"."
- Stephen Fry

"Have you ever heard somebody sing some lyrics that you've never sung before, and you realize you've never sung the right words in that song? You hear them and all of a sudden you say to yourself, 'Life in the Fast Lane?' That's what they're saying right there? You think, 'why have I been singing 'wipe in the vaseline?' how many people have heard me sing 'wipe in the vaseline?' I am an idiot."
- Ellen DeGeneres

"You can put off your dreams, your desires, your careers, your farms. You can avoid your responsibilities, obligations, promises, and sovereign rights. But any person who wants to make music, and doesn't, is a goddamned fool."
- Jenna Woginrich

"With my ninth mind I resurrect my first and dance slow to the music of my soul made new."
- Aberjhani

"What I have achieved by industry and practice, anyone else with tolerable natural gift and ability can also achieve."
- J. S. Bach

"For me, Chanel is like music. There are certain notes and you have to make another tune with them"
- Karl Lagerfeld

"Pop music often tells you everything is OK, while rock music tells you that it's not OK, but you can change it."
- Bono

"Music is the great uniter. An incredible force. Something that people who differ on everything and anything else can have in common."
- Sarah Dessen

"There is music you never hear unless you play it yourself."
- Marty Rubin

"Ruby said there were many songs that you could not say anybody in particular had made by himself. A song went around from fiddler to fiddler and each one added something and took something away so that in time the song became a different thing from what it had been, barely recognizable in either tune or lyric. But you could not say the song had been improved, for as was true of all human effort, there was never advancement. Everything added meant something lost, and about as often as not the thing lost was preferable to the thing gained, so that over time we'd be lucky if we just broke even. Any thought otherwise was empty pride."
- Charles Frazier

"My personal hobbies are reading, listening to music, and silence."
- Edith Sitwell

"I love the relationship that anyone has with music ... because there's something in us that is beyond the reach of words, something that eludes and defies our best attempts to spit it out. ... It's the best part of us probably ..."

- Nick Hornby

"Bruce has always been so nice to me, which is crazy, because he's one of my heroes. I'll never forget being at a Rock and Roll Hall of Fame ceremony the year Bruce and Paul McCartney were inducted. We were at the bar, and Bruce was talking to Paul, and he turned to me and said, 'I can't believe I'm talking to Paul McCartney!' I thought, 'I can't believe I'm talking to Bruce Springsteen, who's talking to Paul McCartney!"
- Melissa Etheridge

"You remember when we were sitting there by the water you put your arm around me for the first time you made a rebel of a careless man's careful daughter you are the best thing that's ever been mine"
- Taylor Swift

"Beethoven tells you what it's like to be Beethoven and Mozart tells you what it's like to be human. Bach tells you what it's like to be the universe."
- Douglas Adams

"I'm not saying I'm gonna change the world, but I guarantee that I will spark the brain that will change the world."
- Tupac Shakur

"Music acts like a magic key, to which the most tightly closed heart opens."
- Maria von Trapp

"You have to, take a deep breath. and allow the music to flow through you. Revel in it, allow yourself to awe. When you play allow the music to break your heart with its beauty."
- Kelly White

"Give me a shot to remember

And you can take all the pain away from me
A kiss and I will surrender
The sharpest lives are the deadliest to lead
A light to burn all the empires
So bright the sun is ashamed to rise and be
And I'm in love with all of those vampires
So you can leave like the sane abandoned me"
- Gerard Way

"I like beautiful melodies telling me terrible things."
- Tom Waits

"The pause makes you think the song will end. And then the song isn't really over, so you're relieved. But then the song does actually end, because every song ends, obviously, and THAT. TIME. THE. END. IS. FOR. REAL."
- Jennifer Egan

"Making a record is a lot like surgery without an anesthetic. You first have to cut yourself up the middle. Then you have to rip out every single organ, every single part and lay them on a table. You then need to examine the parts, and the reality of the situation hits you. You find yourself saying things like "I didn't know that part was so ugly." Or "I better get a professional opinion about that." You go to bed hollow and then back into the operating room the next day. . .facing every fear, every disgusting thing you hate about yourself. Then you pop it all back in, sew yourself shut and perform. . . you perform like your life depended on it----and in those perfect moments you find beauty you never knew existed. You find yourself and you friends all over again, you find something to fight for, something to love. Something to show the world."
- Gerard Way

"I only sing in the shower. I would join a choir, but I don't think my bathtub can hold that many people."
- Jarod Kintz

"The first step - especially for young people with energy and drive and talent, but not money - the first step to controlling your world is to control your culture. To model and demonstrate the kind of world you demand to live in. To write the books. Make the music. Shoot the films. Paint the art."
- Chuck Palahniuk

"Close your eyes and I'll kiss you, Tomorrow I'll miss you."
- Paul McCartney

"I'm telling you a lie in a vicious effort that you will repeat my lie over and over until it becomes true"
- Lady Gaga

"She's not a saint, and she's not what you think
She's an actress, whoa
She's better known for the things that she does on the mattress"
- Taylor Swift

"Some guy said to me: Don't you think you're too old to sing rock n' roll?
I said: You'd better check with Mick Jagger."
- Cher

"I mean, if Beethoven had been killed in a plane crash at twenty-two, the history of music would have been very different. As would the history of aviation, of course."
- Tom Stoppard

"Magic exists. Who can doubt it, when there are rainbows and wildflowers, the music of the wind and the silence of the stars? Anyone who has loved has been touched by magic. It is such a simple and such an extraordinary part of the lives we live."

- Nora Roberts

"Joy, sorrow, tears, lamentation, laughter -- to all these music gives voice, but in such a way that we are transported from the world of unrest to a world of peace, and see reality in a new way, as if we were sitting by a mountain lake and contemplating hills and woods and clouds in the tranquil and fathomless water."
- Albert Schweitzer

"Music is an agreeable harmony for the honor of God and the permissible delights of the soul."
- Johann Sebastian Bach

"Music is an outburst of the soul."
- Frederick Delius

"Music could ache and hurt, that beautiful music was a place a suffering man could hide."
- Pat Conroy

"But when ye come, and all the flowers are dying,
If I am dead, as dead I well may be,
You'll come and find the place where I am lying,
And kneel and say Ave there for me,
And I shall hear, though soft you tread above me,
And all my grave will warmer, sweeter be,
For you will bend and tell me that you love me,
And I shall sleep in peace until you come to me"
- Paul Robeson

"What came first – the music or the misery? Did I listen to the music because I was miserable? Or was I miserable because I listened to the music? Do all those records turn you into a melancholy person?"
- Nick Hornby

"Come along follow me as I lead through the darkness
As I provide just enough spark that we need to proceed
Carry on, give me hope, give me strength
Come with me and I won't steer you wrong
Put your faith and your trust as I guide us through the fog
To the light at the end of the tunnel."
- Eminem

"Would someone care to classify, a broken heart is a twisted
mind so I can find someone to rely on and run to them, to them,
full speed ahead, no you are not useless we are just, Misguided
Ghosts."
- Paramore

"And I'll dance with you in Vienna,
I'll be wearing a river's disguise.
The hyacinth wild on my shoulder
my mouth on the dew of your thighs.
And I'll bury my soul in a scrapbook,
with the photographs there and the moss.
And I'll yield to the flood of your beauty,
my cheap violin and my cross."
- Leonard Cohen

"My heart, which is so full to overflowing, has often been
solaced and refreshed by music when sick and weary."
- Martin Luther

"The tune was sad, as the best of Ireland was, melancholy and
lovely as a lover's tears."
- Nora Roberts

"I am focused on the work. I am constantly creating. I am a busy
girl. I live and breathe my work. I love what I do. I believe in the

message. There's no stopping. I didn't create the fame, the fame created me."
- Lady Gaga

"Sing us a song, and we'll sing it back to you! We could sing our own but what would it be without you! This heart, it beats, beats for only you ."
- Paramore

"V-Day…if you need this one day in a year to show everyone else you truly care for "your loved one" I think it's quite stupid. I hate this commercialism. It's all artificial, and has nothing to do with real love."
- Jess C. Scott

"It is always fatal to have music or poetry interrupted."
- George Eliot

"Next to music beer was best."
- Carson McCullers

"When you've got nothing, you've got nothing to loose."
- Bob Dylan

"Am I the reason you breathe, or am I the reason you cry?"
- Saliva

"Would you destroy Something perfect in order to make it beautiful?"
- Gerard Way

"Sometimes the hardest thing and the right thing are the same…"
- The Fray

"When you were young, and your heart, was an open book. You used to say, live and let live."

- Paul McCartney

"If you cannot teach me to fly, teach me to sing."
- J.M. Barrie

"The music is not in the notes,
but in the silence between."
- Wolfgang Amadeus Mozart

"Who are you to judge the life I live
I know I'm not perfect and I don't live to be, but before you start
pointing fingers make sure your hands are clean."
- Jimi Hendrix

"These times are so hard, and they're getting even harder."
- Eminem

"Men profess to be lovers of music, but for the most part they
give no evidence in their opinions and lives that they have heard
it."
- Henry David Thoreau

"Where words leave off, music begins."
- Heinrich Heine

"Music is the language of the spirit. It opens the secret of life
bringing peace, abolishing strife."
- Kahlil Gibran

"Sometimes I wish Jim Morrison were still alive, because I'd
love to see a concert in which "The Doors" opened up for "The
Cars.""
- Jarod Kintz

"I am no longer afraid of becoming lost, because the journey
back always reveals something new, and that is ultimately good
for the artist."

- Billy Joel

"I've come to the conclusion that people who wear headphones while they walk, are much happier, more confident, and more beautiful individuals than someone making the solitary drudge to work without acknowledging their own interests and power."
- Jason Mraz

"If it weren't for music, I would think that love is mortal."
- Mark Helprin

"Patrick actually used to be popular before Sam bought him some good music."
- Stephen Chbosky

"Well my music was different in high school; I was singing about love—you know, things I don't care about anymore."
- Lady Gaga

"Music is everybody's business. It's only the publishers who think people own it"
- John Lennon

10872507R00080

Printed in Great Britain
by Amazon.co.uk, Ltd.,
Marston Gate.

10872507R00080

Printed in Great Britain
by Amazon.co.uk, Ltd.,
Marston Gate.